BALTI
Curry Cookbook

BALTI
Curry Cookbook

PAT CHAPMAN

PIATKUS

© 1993 Pat Chapman

First published in 1993 by
Judy Piatkus (Publishers) Ltd
5 Windmill Street, London W1P 1HF

**The moral right of the author
has been asserted**

*A catalogue record for this book is available
from the British Library*

ISBN 0 7499 1214 6

Designed by Paul Saunders
Photography by James Murphy
Map on page 8 by Dick Vine
Illustrations by Hanife Hassan O'Keeffe

Special thanks to The Pier, London, for the loan of copper dishes used in the
photograph opposite page 89.

Typeset in 12/13 pt Sabon by
Selwood Systems, Midsomer Norton, Avon
Printed and bound in Great Britain by
Butler & Tanner Ltd, Frome, Somerset

Contents

Foreword

As founder of The Curry Club, I receive, on average, 30 letters a day addressed to me personally, on the subject of curry. That may not sound a lot, but during the course of twelve months it adds up to around 10,000 letters!

The more the merrier. I love it. Firstly, just looking at the stamps and postmarks is fascinating. I usually get at least a couple from overseas. Opening mail is always exciting. What lies within those brown, white, green, pink, or blue envelopes? What information will be there? Will there be something rewarding, entertaining, amusing? About half my mail is from people who have read one of my books and they are requesting more information about The Curry Club. About one third contain reports about curry restaurants. Quite a few people write with specific recipe or ingredient queries. Others send me their favourite recipes, or their travel experiences, and some are just pleasant and chatty. From time to time I get constructive and useful requests and suggestions.

Today's crop is typical: 32 letters including one from Paris, another from Atlanta, Georgia and a third from Kalamunda, Western Australia. Those from the UK include letters from Cardiff, Scunthorpe, Lincoln, Taunton, Manchester, Great Yarmouth and London. All these letters have one thing in common, they're sent in by people who enjoy curry. Like me they are curryholics.

Recently an increasing number of letters have been telling me and asking me about Balti cooking. Two were especially interesting. One came from Berkhamsted, Herts:

Dear Pat,

I would like to purchase a year's subscription to The Curry Club for my brother's birthday. He is a curry addict and is at present sampling his way around all the Balti restaurants in Birmingham, with his friends, every Sunday evening. They started about 18 months ago! But with a family name of Curry (no joke) what can you expect! I know he will be delighted with his birthday present.

Yours sincerely
Gail Burgess (née Curry)

I liked this one so much that I published it in the subsequent edition of *The Curry Club Magazine*. Almost at once Martin Stote, a staff reporter from the *Star* newspaper, was on the phone. He too was fascinated by Balti cooking. How could he get in touch with Gail Burgess's brother? I gave him her full address and Mr Stote tracked down brother Neil and later pronounced that he had a good story for the *Star* which was duly published. (Neil, incidentally, is now a full member of The Curry Club.)

The other letter arrived just as I finished the manuscript of this book, and I was turning my thoughts to writing the introduction. It came from Mr Ian Pettigrew who lives near Edinburgh. Without realising it, he too is putting in a request for a Balti cookbook.

Dear Pat,

I enjoyed our brief chat with you last month at the excellent curry evening which you put on at Lancer's Restaurant, Edinburgh.

As a practising curryholic, I could eat the stuff every night, but a proper curry meal, with an abundance of side dishes, and all the preparation it entails, is just not on for the small family on a tight budget with babies to bath and not a lot of time.

How about more, 'all-in-one' curry recipes (authentic ones) incorporating meat/poultry/fish cooked with potatoes/lentils etc.

How about it, Pat? Don't condemn me to an eternity of mid-week pizza!

Keep it up.

Ian Pettigrew.

By definition Balti recipes are just what you asked for Ian: all-in-one curries. They are also relatively quick to prepare. With a little bit of preparation and judicious use of the freezer, Balti cooking is stir-fried to a rapid conclusion. Some meat dishes and certain base sauces can be pre-prepared in batches and kept in the freezer and just thawed and finished off 'on the day'. Once the sauce bases are prepared and to hand, most of the dishes in this book can be put together in 20–30 minutes.

The beauty of Balti is that you can combine any ingredient with any other, if you wish. Often this decision is simply made for you by what you have in stock. 'Mix'n'match' is the order of the day. So any dishes from Chapters 2–5 can be combined. Chapter 7 gives some examples to start you off.

This book's 100 or so recipes concentrate only on main-course dishes in the categories of meat, poultry, fish and vegetables. For completeness (of the main course), I have included a few accompaniments such as rice, breads and chutneys. There are no starters or desserts. Those who want such items will find them in my other curry books (see page ii).

This book goes back to the roots of Balti cooking and incorporates many unusual and authentic Pakistani recipes which I have been fortunate enough to collect on my travels. It also includes the techniques and recipes from the modern UK Balti restaurant. I have converted both of these cooking styles to home-cooking techniques.

So, dedicated to Gail Burgess, Neil Curry, the Pettigrews and babes, and all curryholics wherever you are, here is my *Balti Curry Cookbook*. I hope Ian will find it an indispensable alternative to his mid-week pizza. Indeed I hope it will appeal to all curryholics, some as yet to be converted. As the Balti movement grows up and down Great Britain and beyond, maybe we'll even coin a new word for people with a passion for this kind of food, and the *Baltiholic* will be born.

So don't forget to write to me telling of your curry experiences (but please don't forget an SAE, if you want a reply):

Pat Chapman,
The Curry Club,
PO BOX 7
Haslemere,
Surrey
GU27 1EP

Introduction

There really are Balti people who live in Baltistan. Once it was a kingdom complete with its own royals. Now it is the northernmost part of Pakistan. It is located on the roof of the world and though few places are as remote and inhospitable, few people are more friendly and few have such a colourful history. Their food has evolved over centuries into pan-cooked stir-fries and slow-cooked dryish stews. The results are aromatic and very tasty indeed.

It was an imaginative restaurateur who, by establishing a Balti restaurant in, of all places, Birmingham, a few years ago, put Balti cooking on the map. It took off in a big way and just ten years later there are no less than 100 Balti houses in Birmingham with dozens more springing up all over the country.

Here is the fascinating background to the Balti curry trend which is sweeping the British Isles in the 1990s in the way that tandoori did two decades earlier.

WHAT IS BALTI?

'Seriously delicious' is how Patrick, Earl of Lichfield, described Balti cooking when he first encountered it in 1992 at the **Royal Naweed** Balti restaurant in Moseley, in the company of the *Birmingham Post*'s Carol Ann Rice.

Balti is a type of Kashmiri curry whose origins go back centuries in the area which is now north Pakistan. It became established in England in 1975 when a new breed of restaurant, the Balti house, opened in a Birmingham suburb, since when it has mushroomed in that area and beyond. Balti refers both to its area of origin and the

1

dish in which the food is cooked and served to the table. Known also as the *karahi*, the Balti pan is a round-bottomed, wok-like, heavy cast-iron dish with two handles. The foods served in the Balti pan are freshly cooked aromatically spiced curries. Balti food at its best is very aromatic but not excessively spiked with chillies. Traditionally it is eaten without rice or cutlery. Balti bread is used to scoop up the food using the right hand only.

The origins of Balti cooking are wide ranging and owe as much to China (with a slight resemblance to the spicy cooking of Szechuan) and Tibet as to the tribal ancestry of the nomad, the tastes of the Moghul emperors, the aromatic spices of Kashmir, and the 'winter foods' of lands high in the mountains. Balti food is both simple in its concept and cooking, and complex in its flavours. True Balti food is dryish and slightly oily and spicily tasty. The modern British Balti house has retained the traditional concepts and has widened the range of Balti to encompass many favourite curries which have never been heard of in Baltistan. A glance through Chapter 6 will show you what I mean.

Whether this modification of the authentic and traditional is a good thing or a bad thing, is frankly, I believe, irrelevant. The diners at a Birmingham Balti house have as much in common with a Balti or Pathan tribesman as an alien from outer space. Indeed many of the Balti house owners and workers have probably been no nearer to Baltistan than their customers. Their demands are quite different.

So too are those of householders who want to cook at home. In Baltistan they cook what they cook, day by day, meal by meal according to what provisions they have in store. Most of us at home do the same for our lunch, tea, supper or dinner. Unless we are planning an elaborate entertaining session, we simply use what we've got. In this respect Balti cooking is perfect.

In this book I give recipes for the two types of Balti cooking – authentic recipes from Baltistan, and recipes for Balti dishes as served in the modern Balti restaurant.

THE BALTI RESTAURANT

The first Birmingham Balti restaurants, or houses, were, in effect, curry transport cafés. Furnishings were basic. Formica chairs and tables were bolted to the floor. They stayed open from 10 am to 3 am daily and you paid in advance. A wide choice of dishes were offered, all called Balti this and Balti that: Balti Meat, Balti Chicken, Balti Prawns, Balti Vegetables, Balti Dhals. All could be ordered in any combination – so Balti Meat with Peas, or Balti Chicken with Carrots, or Balti Prawns with Chickpeas or Balti Meat with Chicken or Balti Prawns with Meat were just some examples on the original menu. The choice was up to the diner. Spicing was subtle with an emphasis on fresh garlic, ginger, coriander leaf and aromatic spices including clove, cassia bark, cardamoms, aniseed, fennel, cummin and garam masala. As the restaurateurs were Pakistani Moslems, alcohol was not served and the Balti house not licensed.

As time went by, clones began to open around the Midlands. By the mid 1980s, things began to elaborate and menus got longer with some restaurants offering over 60 Balti dishes. The combinations have became legendary. **Adil's**, one of the earliest Balti houses, offers such coded delights as Balti Mt-Spi-Cha-Chi-Aub, meaning Balti meat with spinach, chana dhal, chickpeas and aubergine. Another favourite is Balti Tropical which is a combination of Balti meat, chicken and prawns. The ultimate mix is called The Exhausting Balti Dish by at least two Balti houses (**Azims** and the **Royal Watan**). I asked one of the waiters why it was called 'Exhausting'. 'Simple', he said in a perfect Kashmiri Brum accent, 'it will exhaust you eating it!' A better epitaph I cannot write.

The secrets of the Balti houses are their Balti house sauces and individual spicings. With these they can create any curry favourite dishes in any combination. I reveal these secrets to you in this book, so that you can recreate at home your favourite Balti dishes.

Balti is fun. The Balti houses and their supporters know this but its true supporters take Balti very seriously. And there are some extremely serious supporters. Take, for example, Andy Munro who edits a small guide to Birmingham's Balti houses under the title *The Essential Street Balti Guide*. He is probably the country's foremost Balti house expert, and has his own criteria for the ideal Balti house which he related to me over the telephone in his rich fruity Brum accent:

'The place should be unpretentious but clean. Dress can be as informal or as formal as you wish. Booking should not be necessary. The food should be inexpensive, starter and main course with bread being under £6. The diner should have an unrestricted amount of choice of combinations of mix'n' match ingredients. The food should be freshly cooked. Spices should have '*street credibility*' – they should be subtle not pungent hot.

It should take no more than 15 minutes to serve. The food should come to the table in sizzling black Balti pans. The Balti house should be unlicensed and they should not object to nor charge for diners bringing their own alcohol.'

Munro admits that there are some Balti houses that have gone 'up-market' in decor and location and are licensed which means a higher price tag, and whilst he tolerates this trend and even dines in such establishments, he clearly disapproves.

He has his own top five – **The Punjab Paradise**, Ladypool Road; **The Royal Naim**, Stratford Road; the **Sher Khan**, Stratford Road; **The Ib-ne-Ghani**, Bordesely Green and the quaintly named **I am the King of Balti**, Ladypool Road. He even claims he would be able to tell one restaurant's food from another 'blindfold'. Yes, Andy Munro and his fellow addicts take Balti very seriously. They call themselves 'Balti maniacs'!

Get amongst them and you'll find yourself immersed in Balti legends and endless arguments about which was the first Balti house and which is the best. They talk of the 'Balti triangle' being that area within Brum's mystical eastern suburbs, centred around Sparkbrook, where Balti began. They refer to Balti naan breads as being *'as light as, and the same shape as a duvet'*. (One almost expects them to refer to their tog weight.) They call Stoney Lane the *'Balti Run'*, and Lye near Wolverhampton the *'Balti capital of the Black Country'*. They refer to Birmingham's Bristol Street as *'Spice Alley'*, which must not, of course be confused with **Spice Avenue**, a new upmarket Balti house in the middle of the Balti triangle, which Andy Munro reckons *'is rather like discovering the New York Hilton in Beirut, where they even "flaboyed"* (sic. **Spice Avenue**) *the Balti specials in brandy at a predictably five star price!'*

Other curiosities they discuss include a restaurant called **The Falcon** (called, as you might guess, the **'Baltese Falcon'** by the local Balti-philes), and **Balti Towers** of which the cognoscenti say there is no sign of Basil except in the spices. The extremists even boast that they breakfast on Balti (at the **Minar**, Sparkbrook which opens at 9 am on Sundays).

Just which restaurant was the first Balti house is now as much a topic of fierce argument amongst Balti maniacs and Balti res-taurateurs as is the origin of species amongst learned anthro-pologists. And so serious is the debate that one might consider that *Homo erectus* and *sapiens* had less importance than *Homo Balti*.

The honours go, according to the King of Balti himself, Andy

Munro, to the incongruously named **Paris** restaurant in Alum Rock Road, Saltley, whose owner, one Mr Ramzan, was 'unavailable for comment' during the entire time I was researching this book. It appears Mr Ramzan was born and bred in the northernmost area of Pakistan and brought his native food back to England to start a restaurant.

Rather more available for comment and certainly more intent on claiming the crown is Mohammed Arif, who with his brother Ashraf runs the two celebrated **Adil's** restaurants, both of which are situated in Birmingham's Stoney Lane, Moseley. A couple of miles south east of New Street station, it is now the centre of British Balti Land, along with neighbouring Sparkbrook and Sparkhill. In this area alone there are no less than 40 Balti houses ranging from tiny, cosy, unlicensed one-man-band establishments to the luxurious empires with a huge complement of staff and a massive turnabout of customers.

Whether the first was the Paris or Adil's probably matters little. Mohammed Arif says he got the idea. His restaurant opened in 1975 or 76, a year or two after the Paris, but he is adamant that Balti was his idea. '*My grandfather ran a restaurant in Kashmir called Adil (meaning "Justice"),*' says Arif. '*Customers there picked their own raw ingredients and watched the entire cooking process. Apart from that, in all other respects, the cooking at our Adil's restaurant is identical.*' Ashraf learned to cook there and in 1969, he and his brother came to England to join their father, who by now worked in a restaurant in Bradford. When they settled in Birmingham, the idea to set up a new Adil's seemed the best thing to do. Adil's restaurant soon became popular and a second branch opened nearby on the same street.

In 1991 I was asked by BBC Birmingham Radio to suggest a good curry venue for a late night chat show. I suggested Balti at Adil's and a complete BBC outside broadcast unit was set up on the first floor of the restaurant.

Adil's is a typical Balti house. It is unlicensed, very busy and enormously popular. Glass tops cover the menus on each table. Animated conversation is punctuated by the regular clatter and hiss of steel Balti pans being served by the energetic staff. A peep into the kitchen reveals a hive of activity and a monster stock of Balti pans, waiting alongside the gas stoves and tandoori ovens. Tantalising smells impregnate all areas. Diner anticipation is intense. Their chatter is inexhaustible. The fun is endless.

My intention is that this cookbook gives you just as much fun, taking Balti out of the restaurant and for the first time bringing it into the home, revealing Balti's innermost secrets, its subtleties, its tasty flavours, its aromatics and its aromas.

In the 1970s it was tandoori cooking which captured the imagination of the British diner and within a decade, every curry restaurant up and down the land offered tandoori dishes whether or not they possessed a tandoor. Two decades later it is Balti cooking which is set to expand nationwide. It is already to be found as far afield as Cardiff, Southampton and Northumberland. Even Marks and Spencer, the UK's number-one food supermarket chain, have introduced pre-chilled, ready-cooked Balti dishes to their curry ranges. London has yet to open its first Balti house, but it will undoubtedly come, and after it will follow many others.

Before that time you will have enjoyed working your way through this book.

I recently appeared on a British Forces Broadcasting Services radio programme with Lord Lichfield. I actually cooked a Balti dish on radio, and Lord Lichfield re-affirmed his view that Balti was 'seriously delicious'.

I hope you'll agree after you've cooked some of these recipes.

Before we come to the recipes themselves, let's take a look at the colourful history of Balti – the place and its people as opposed to the modern restaurant and its food.

THE BALTI LANDS AND PEOPLE

The northernmost part of the sub-continent is literally on the 'roof of the world'. It is called Baltistan, and is in Pakistan in the area they call the Upper Northern Territories. At latitude 36°N and longtitude 74°E, with an area of 10,000 square miles, Baltistan is sandwiched between the world's highest mountain ranges – the Himalayas, the Karakorams and the Hindu Kush. Pakistan's highest mountain, K2 (at 28,250 feet the second highest in the world), is just one of many mountains in the range peaking over 23,000 feet. The average valley height is 9,000 feet. Winters are severe. The area is literally cut off from the rest of the world for months on end. The air pressure is low, oxygen is short and water boils at 70°C.

It is, to put it mildly, one of the most elusive, toughest places on earth to dwell. Yet people do. They have done so for many centuries. In fact Baltistan's valleys are extremely fertile, assisted by the mighty River Indus, which flows through Baltistan on its way from Tibet to the Arabian Sea near Pakistan's second city, Karachi. Called the Father of Rivers, the Indus flows for 2,560 miles (3,300 km), and has always been of major importance to the region. Some 1,000 miles south of Baltistan, it caused the plains of Pakistan to become extremely fertile and become home to Palaeolithic man 500,000 years ago.

By 2,800 BC, the world's third literate society had evolved there. Archaeologists only discovered the evidence of this society early this century and called them the Indus Valley Civilisation after the great river. Well preserved remains of cities, complete with hot and cold running water systems and drainage, have been found at Harappa and Mohenjo-Daro. These people became as advanced as the two literate civilisations on the Mediterranean, the Egyptians and the Mesopotamians. Indeed they traded together exchanging, amongst other things, spices and food ingredients.

Access to the Indus Valley had nearly always been through narrow mountain passes from the west. The most celebrated of these is the Khyber Pass. From the earliest days nomadic tribes passed through here in search of territories which would enable their expanding populations to grow. Tribes became civilised and hunters became organised soldiers, their leaders kings. Armies came through the pass to conquer and pillage and obtain wealth. And so it was, with the arrival through the Khyber Pass of a major tribe of wandering dairy herdsmen, the Aryans, that by 800 BC the Indus Valley Civilisation was wiped out. The Aryans left no archaeological remains of their own. As nomads they did not need buildings and structures. The legacy the Aryans left was much more significant. Their dairy herds became venerated, the cow became sacred. They established Hinduism and they gave the name of India to the country they had conquered. For nearly 1,000 years the Aryans were left to establish their culture.

Later the Khyber Pass gave entry to Persian invaders who colonised the Indus Valley and then, under Alexander the Great, it became Greek. A succession of conquerors came and went including Buddhists, Cushians, Huns and more Persians. But it was the Arabs who, by the eighth century AD, established Islam in the area, and put down roots which prevail to this day.

Following the dispersal of the Jews from Israel a tribe called the Pathans became nomadic. Eventually they came upon the Khyber Pass, found the land beyond to their liking and settled there. Pale skinned and blue eyed, they became Moslems. They are the present

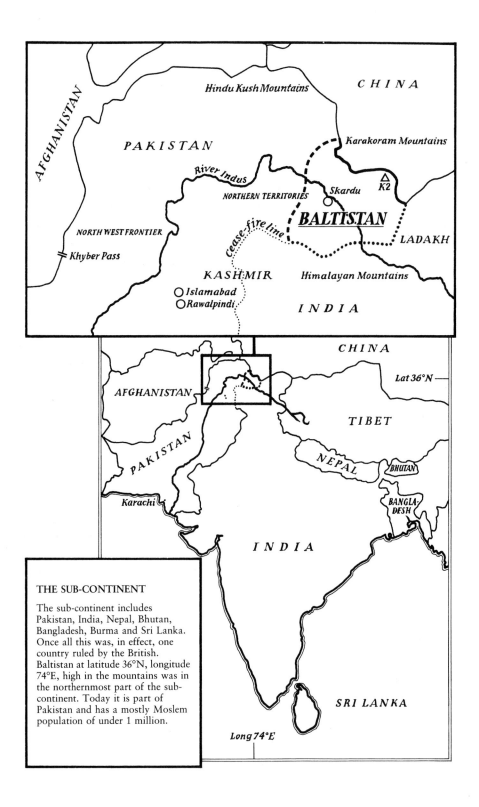

AFGHANISTAN

Hindu Kush Mountains

CHINA

PAKISTAN

Karakoram Mountains

River Indus

NORTHERN TERRITORIES

Skardu

△ K2

BALTISTAN

LADAKH

Cease-fire line

NORTH WEST FRONTIER

═ Khyber Pass

KASHMIR

Himalayan Mountains

○ Islamabad
○ Rawalpindi

INDIA

CHINA

Lat 36°N

AFGHANISTAN

TIBET

PAKISTAN

NEPAL

BHUTAN

Karachi

BANGLA-
DESH

INDIA

THE SUB-CONTINENT

The sub-continent includes
Pakistan, India, Nepal, Bhutan,
Bangladesh, Burma and Sri Lanka.
Once all this was, in effect, one
country ruled by the British.
Baltistan at latitude 36°N, longitude
74°E, high in the mountains was in
the northernmost part of the sub-
continent. Today it is part of
Pakistan and has a mostly Moslem
population of under 1 million.

SRI LANKA

Long 74°E

day incumbents of the region remaining primitive, fierce and aggressive.

Islam was reinforced in the sixteeth century when Babur, the first Moghul Emperor, came through the Khyber Pass and conquered the sub-continent and established a dynasty that was to last for three centuries, until little by little it disintegrated allowing the British traders of the East India Company to take control of the whole of the sub-continent.

The legendary Khyber Pass is surely known to nearly everyone, if for no better reason than epic and comic movies. The Carry On comedy team gave it a kind of status in the 70s, mixing metaphors with clichés and British soldiers in red coats and white pith helmets with be-turbanned natives. There is an element of truth in these images, and certainly the British regarded the Khyber Pass as a keystone to the security of India.

The Khyber Pass is a narrow natural passage way which literally connects Afghanistan to Pakistan. It winds its way for 50 miles (80 km) or so with towering vertical mountains, some 3,300 feet (1,000 metres) high, converging until at a single point the mountains are just 50 feet (16 metres) apart.

The British gave the area the apt name the North West Frontier. Because of the Khyber Pass, the area was one of major strategic importance for the British, and as with all previous and subsequent governments they found it a turbulent and troublesome area to control. The Pathans were unpredictable and the pressures of Moslem versus Hindu never abated. The British coped, as they did with the 640 cantankerous Maharajas all over the sub-continent. The area was of little commercial value, but with the continual threat of a Russian invasion from the west, the British installed a thorough system of rail, roads and telegraphs, to ensure they had instant communications and potentially rapid troop movement in the area.

To the north of the North West Frontier was an even more inhospitable area, high in the mountains, which the British named the Northern Territories. It had even less commercial value to the British than the North West Frontier lands. It did however hold a potential threat of invasion from the north through the mountains from China.

The Spice Route

At the time of the birth of Christ, the Chinese had established a trading route which linked China's then capital, Xian, on its eastern seaboard, with her nearest trading nations, India and the kingdoms of the Mediterranean. From end to end the route was 6,000 miles (9,654 km), traversing deserts, mountains, forests and steppes and linking ancient fortified major cities all along the way. The main route passed from Xian to Zhedgzhou in China, across central Asia to Kashgar and Samarkard then on to Baghdad, Damascus and Cairo. China's principal exports were beautifully crafted artifacts in jade, bronze and lacquered wood, and furs, dried fruit, nuts and valuable spices such as cassia bark. By far the most prolific export was Chinese silk and it was not surprising therefore that the route became known as the Silk Route or Road. The Chinese obtained horses, along with gold, silver, ivory, jewels, coral, glass, walnuts, almonds, broad beans, onions, cucumbers and grapes and spices such as pepper and cummin.

By 100 AD the Silk Route was at its height supplying the Roman Empire. It was incredibly busy with endless loads of goods travelling in both directions The Chinese merchant in Xian city would sell his merchandise to a middleman, and so on up and down the line. The network was populated with a chain of merchants, agents and middlemen, culminating at the western end with Arab traders. It took over two years for the goods to traverse the route from one end to the other, although few people would actually do the journey from end to end and back again. Marco Polo, the fifteenth century Venetian explorer, traversed it in both directions during his 16-year exploration of the known world. One branch of the Silk Route turned south through the Karakoram mountains and passed through Baltistan on its way to India and the Khyber Pass. This diversion became known as the Spice Route.

The first settlers in Baltistan were nomads from Tibet. Primitive rock carvings have been found depicting scenes of hunters with ibex, lynx and snow leopards. Before the birth of Christ, the area had become a centre of Buddhism. Indeed it is likely that it was from here that Buddhism entered China. Baltistan was important for the selection, education and development of Lamas (Tibetan holy monks). Later, Hindu nomadic tribes moved here. The establishment of the Spice Route led to Chinese supremacy in Baltistan for several hundred years then power tipped between China, Tibet and Ladakh until the fifteenth century.

It was then that Moslem invaders bought Islam to Baltistan. Shortly after that the Spice and Silk routes declined as Portuguese and later British colonisers achieved maritime supremacy of the world's trading routes.

Nineteenth and Twentieth Century Baltistan

Baltistan never became a part of the Moghul empire but the British recognised that leaving remote Baltistan unguarded could be the thin edge of a Chinese invasionary wedge. It was, after all, in exactly this way that the British precipitated the decline of the Moghul empire, by establishing British outposts in places the Moghuls took no interest in such as Madras, Calcutta and Bombay. So the upper Northern Territories were brought under the control of the British civil and military administrators in the nineteenth century, for strategic reasons. Railways were impractical in the mountainous territory but they built a few narrow roads and stationed troops there. These were mostly Hindu Sikh troops, reflecting the racial background of the neighbouring Maharaja of Kashmir, whom the British allowed to be nominal royal ruler of the area.

The pressure for independence grew progressively stronger during the twentieth century, until it exploded in 1947 with the violent separation of a newly created Pakistan from India – Moslem from Hindu. At this time Kashmir and Baltistan was under the nominal rule of the Maharaja of Kashmir, Hari Sing. He was one of three Indian princes to vasicilate over whether to place his state with Pakistan or India. He was a Hindu and his people mostly Moslem. He avidly hoped that by remaining neutral, his kingdom would become independent. Whilst he sat on the fence, fiercely Moslem Pathan tribesmen decided to take the law into their own hands and they invaded the area from the west in a bloody ravage, in the name of Islam. The Indian government retaliated by sending in troops from the south. The result was a stand off, punctuated to this day in sporadic fighting over the disputed border, the 'cease fire line' at which Baltistan and Kashmir are the buffers.

The few roads that joined Indian Kashmir to Baltistan are now closed. What towns there are, are isolated and spread out along a single road to the east which peters out long before the border. So remote and unguarded is the region, that the Chinese built a complete highway in the neighbouring Indian state of Ladakh without the Indians noticing. This resulted in the Indo-Chinese border war and the loss to India of northern Ladakh.

With the agreement of Pakistan, the Chinese also constructed the Karakoram Highway, which enters the Upper Northern Territories through a newly re-opened pass from Chinese Tibet and runs down the Indus Valley adjacent to the Silk Route along the western edge of the state of Baltistan, and on into the lowlands of Pakistan.

The People and Way of Life

Whilst the Indus Valley drew wave after wave of settlers over the millennia, lured there by its fertility, the hostility of Baltistan's terrain caused it to be less attractive. The first settlers were purely nomadic. Later they began to cultivate land and eventually, they settled founding towns and fortresses.

I recently met a sixty year old Punjabi, whose father had lived in the area as a boy. The man told me of how the Balti had lived until quite recently.

Basically they were survivors – nomads who carried their worldly possessions on their backs. They didn't have cows, rather they relied on catching passing wild goats. '*A cow must be milked twice a day*', the man told me. '*A goat you can milk any time of the day or night and as many times as you like. Catching one is easier than tethering it and bringing it with you – then you have to find food for it.*' As for cooking he said that you cooked what you caught or picked. '*Dried dung cakes provided the fuel. Any kind of dung is OK,*' he said. '*What ever turns up, use it.*'

The food was cooked in a round bottomed cooking pan and that was the only thing you carried with you as you '*preambled on your travels*'. The cooking pan they most probably used was the Chinese wok, brought to the area along the Silk Route. It is conceivable that cooking with a rounded bottom pan spread from here to the whole sub-continent of India and back again, giving rise to the two handled **karahi** or the **balti pan** which is distinct from but similar to the wok.

Today's Balti people are no longer nomadic, but combine the many racial roots which the last two thousand years have forced upon them. They are pale skinned and resemble Tibetans in facial appearance and dress. Their languages comprise many dialects and their architecture resembles that of Tibet.

For many months of the year the weather closes the place down in a blanket of snow and ice, and a howl of wind. Despite this, and despite being in a war zone, Baltis are cheerful and resilient.

Their spring and summer is delightful and at times the temperature can peak at 35°C. Autumn is mild, but the winds start to get going. The valleys are very fertile and produce grows quite rapidly in the summer enabling Baltistan to be virtually self sufficient for food stuffs. They grow rice, wheat, barley, maize and millet and apples, apricots, blackberries, gooseberries, peaches, pears, and walnuts are prolific in season. Vegetables include asparagus, beans, carrots, lentils, onions, peas, potatoes, radish, turnips, watercress and ten varieties of mushrooms. These are dried and stored for the long winter.

Dairy products are universal from the female ox (the *dri*). Meat comes from yak, and buffalo of Chinese origin. A hybrid is called the *dzo* and its young, the *a-ko*, is popular for meat. Goats also provide meat and milk. Fresh water fishing is good from the River Indus and its many tributaries and large and small game, flighted and non-flighted, is widespread and plentiful. Until recently there were no restrictions on hunting the ibex, lynx, markhar and musk deer so it is not surprising that these have now become extremely rare. The snow leopard is also hunted – it is regarded as a pest and it is quite prolific. Game birds small and large are also prolific, the most popular of which is partridge (*chi kor*). Domestic chickens are valuable and relatively expensive.

A visit to the area involves considerable effort. There is one flight a day, weather permitting, between Rawalpindi and the tiny air field at Skardu, the capital of Baltistan, aboard a Pakistan Airlines 48-seat piston-engined F27 Fokker aircraft. It is an exhilarating hour-long hop, dodging mountain peaks. The alternative is a four-day uncomfortable jeep drive. Tourists are rare at Skardu, but they are made very welcome by the exceptionally friendly Baltis. There is a hotel and a restaurant there, and hospitality cannot be bettered.

For those wishing to travel on towards the Indian border, the most reliable form of transport is the yak or mule. The road peters out after a few miles and there is little to see. Of course it is now impossible to cross into Indian Kashmir. Indeed it is a similar story on the other side of the border. One must fly to Srinagar from Delhi then take a jeep as close as you can go to the border. It is not a journey most of us will take.

But the advent of the Balti house and the excellence which is Balti and Kashmiri cooking is now available to everyone through the pages of this book.

CHAPTER 1

The Balti Workshop

This chapter enables you to tackle any of the recipes in this book by ensuring that you have the right equipment to hand, and by taking you through a number of techniques and ingredients important to Balti curry cooking. So, before you begin to cook the Balti recipes in the subsequent chapters, I recommend that you read this chapter carefully, followed by Appendix 2, in which I detail further ingredients important in Balti cookery.

BASIC EQUIPMENT

The Balti Pan

Balti cooking is very ancient, and relies on few implements. The original cast-iron pot, the Balti, used for slow cooking above the embers of the camp fire, can be replaced by a Balti frying pan. This is to Balti cooking what the wok is to Chinese. It is probable that the idea was brought from China along the ancient Silk Route (see page 10) across the Karakoram Pass and into Baltistan, evolving into a slightly deeper, more rounded pan, and becoming one of the sub-continent's main cooking implements. Known variously as the *karahi*, or *kari, korai, kadai* or *kodoi*, it is a circular two-handled, hemispherical, all-purpose cooking pan used for stir-frying, simmering, frying and deep-frying – in fact it is highly efficient for all types of pan cooking. Sizes range from massive (over 3 ft 3 in/1 metre in diameter) to small (as little as 3¼ in/8 cm). Small ones are used to serve food in and the Balti tradition is to cook in them and serve them straight to the table. If you do not yet possess a wok or a karahi you can use, of course, frying pans, although these lack finesse of control, and the authenticity which is part of the fun of Balti cooking.

The traditional material for the Balti pan was cast iron, making them quite heavy. Today they are pressed from chromium vanadium steel, which makes them thin but sturdy. To cater for modern cookers, the ancient rounded bottom has been flattened to make the pan stable on top of the modern stove. A wok makes a perfect substitute and those with a long single handle are actually easier to use.

You will need at least one large Balti karahi or wok of about 14 in (35 cm) in diameter. I also like to use small karahi or woks of 6–7 in (15–17.5 cm) in diameter for single-portion or small item work. Big ones take up a lot of space on the stove, two being the maximum you can use at once. Smaller ones give you greater flexibility.

So my complement is two large and two small Balti karahi or woks (but see also serving ideas on page 23).

Preparing a New Balti Pan

A new one needs cleaning with a non abrasive sink cleaning cream to remove the lacquer or machine oil applied by the manufacturers to prevent rust. After that rinse it several times in hot water. Then place it on a heated ring on the stove for a minute or so. This dries it out for the next stage.

Seasoning a Balti Pan

This starts the build up of a protective film on the pan, which, over time, builds up to create a non-stick finish.

Place about 3 or 4 tablespoons cooking oil (old used cooking oil is acceptable) in the pan, heat it to smoking point, and swirl it around. Allow to cool, then pour it out and wipe the pan clean with kitchen paper.

Cleaning a Balti Pan

It should never be scoured clean. To do so would be to lose the blackened patina that builds up over time, and which is said to improve the flavour of the food being cooked. Indeed the Chinese say of a cook, 'the blacker the wok, the better the cook'.

It is true that a blackened pan looks the part, but (sacrilege!) I honestly cannot tell the difference between using a new well-scoured pan and my old well-blackened (and I'm sure less hygienic) one. However, the best tool to use to clean the pan without scratching it or losing the patina is a Chinese wok brush. This is a fairly substantial item with a firm round handle and a number of stout bamboo bristles. It cleans the pan effectively, but it then takes a fair bit of cleaning itself.

Items to Use with a Balti Pan

The modern wok has a number of items of associated equipment which work just as well with the Balti karahi pan. It has a steel stand on which to place it when off the stove. It has a well-fitting domed lid. Also available is a wok spatula – a steel scraper whose blade is shaped to fit snugly to the curve of the wok. Two ladles are designed to work with the wok, one perforated, the other not.

Obtaining Balti Equipment

Your Balti meals can be cooked using conventional western sauce-pans and frying pans – although I sincerely believe that much of the fun comes from the noisy clattering of a large chef's spoon in a Balti pan.

The fun extends to your guests if you serve Balti in small Balti serving dishes, especially if they sizzle from pan to table (don't forget to use a wooden base unless you want to have burn marks all over your table). See page 136 for instructions.

All this specialist equipment can be found at some Asian stores. Easier still, use The Curry Club's mail-order service of which details appear in Appendices 1 and 2, pages 148–50.

Other Equipment

You will also need the following common kitchen utensils and tools to cook Balti.

knives
chopping boards
mixing bowls (non-metallic, large, medium and small)
large sieve
large chef's spoon for stir-frying
large flat frying pan or *tava* (Indo-Pak griddle pan)
saucepans with lids (6 pint/3.5 litre, 4 pint/2.25 litre,
    2¹/₄ pint/1.3 litre)
oven tray(s)
grill tray with wire rack
bamboo steamer, 8 in (20 cm), or a metal steamer

a large frying pan with perforated inner pan and a tight-fitting lid (a colander or strainer over a pan with a lid will substitute)

a sprung-type mechanical vegetable chopper (this saves work and is very much cheaper than the electric equivalents)

Electrical Tools

Although many of these items are expensive, and take up a lot of space, it is with these tools that we can save time.

Blender
The device for making purées requiring some liquid and which achieves the correct texture for curries.

Food Processor
An expensive but immensely useful kitchen tool. Its standard blade can be used to make purées, although even with added water they are not of as fine a texture as those made in a blender. Other blades include vegetable shredders and slicers.

Coffee Grinder
An effective way to grind spices. It can handle most spices and grind them reasonably finely. Best results are obtained when the spices are 'roasted' (see page 30) and cooled first, and the machine is not loaded past the half-way mark. A damp wipe leaves the machine ready to handle coffee beans without tainting them.

Spice Mill
A new attachment for 'Chef' units which grinds all spices, raw or roasted, to any degree of fineness you want.

Dough Hook Attachment
A great time and effort saver if you make bread.

Rice Cooker
In my view, a total extravagance. But if you want one or have one, then use it and you'll get good results.

Warming Drawer
In Chapter 7, I mention the use of a warming drawer. Some ovens have these, but if yours doesn't, use the oven itself on its lowest setting.

Microwave

A much maligned kitchen tool, the microwave seems to be regarded by some as the enemy of real cooking. I've heard people say that 'real' restaurants or cooks would not use a microwave. This is rubbish, of course. It gets its poor reputation as the purveyor of soggy pub pies, a role in which it performs at its worst. The microwave is a high-speed cooker with limitations.

Like the food processor, it is invaluable in some roles and useless in others. It is great for fast thawing of frozen foods, for casseroling and for reheating wet dishes. It boils water fast and is excellent for blanching vegetables, and it cooks papadoms. But in my experience, it does not handle the initial frying (*bargar*) of spices and purées effectively, and it is hopeless for cooking or reheating pastry.

Microwaves vary in power from 350 watts to 2,000 watts (the latter being ultra-powerful, very fast catering units), the average being 650 watts. Cooking time depends on the power of your particular machine, so again your own experience is your best guide. I'm not absolutely sold on the common theory that micro-waving detracts from flavours. There seems to be no scientific reason for it.

KEEPING BALTI

By definition Balti should be freshly cooked. However, we are bound to get surplus items or 'leftovers' which it would be ridiculous to throw away.

Always use a refrigerator to store cooked Balti and always ensure that the food is cold first. Putting warm food into the fridge raises the temperature inside the fridge whilst the heat exchange motor struggles to bring the temperature back down. You can thus introduce the risk of causing food already in the fridge to go off.

The texture and the flavour of the dishes will change. Meat and poultry will appear slightly blander, because the spices have marinated into the ingredients. Vegetables will go softer.

Providing that you know that the raw ingredients used to cook the Balti dish were absolutely fresh, not pre-frozen, and were cooked immediately after purchase, and cooled rapidly after cooking, covered and placed in the fridge as soon as it became cold then it is safe to store the dish in the fridge for up to 48 hours. Even so 48 hours is a long time even in a fridge. Freezing is a much safer method of storing.

Freezing

The freezer is one of the West's wonder electrical tools. It is not available in Pakistan and the curry lands, except for an elite wealthy few (even the fridge is rare over there). But to the western householder, it is a mandatory item on the inventory. Like the fridge, it too has its uses and drawbacks.

The main point about home freezing is to preserve seasonal items for use out of season. I like to do this with some things and not with others. I prefer to freeze my own sweetcorn – it tastes so much better than the commercial versions. On the other hand I think bought frozen peas are in many cases better than home-frozen ones. You can freeze fruit and vegetables raw, exactly as they are when picked or purchased (cleaning and discarding unwanted matter first). I often do this, but the textbooks advise that you should cook the subject matter first, at least blanch it, to remove bacteria and gasses. It's up to you.

Freezing comes into its own with the preservation of cooked foods and it is ideal for Balti bases and sauces, and for some complete dishes. Freezing will change the taste of a curry – it's like a long marination. It will soften meats and vegetables and tends to intensify certain whole aromatic spices, though the overall taste will become blander.

Here are a few common-sense freezer observations:

1. Use only fresh ingredients, not items that have come from the freezer.

2. Choose your subject carefully. Some ingredients are not suitable for freezing. Items with a high water content change markedly in structure when they thaw, their texture becoming unpleasant.

   Meat and poultry are excellent, as are all lentil dishes. Some vegetables work well – aubergines, peas, beans, carrots and mashed potatoes for example. Most soft fruit and vegetables are not as successful.

   Fish and seafood work well. Rice is satisfactory but I can never see the point – it takes so little time to make fresh rice (and it has better taste and texture).

3. Always undercook a dish destined for the freezer by about 10 minutes to allow for 'tenderising' in the freezing process and reheating. (This does not apply to sauce bases.)

4. Take out any large whole spices before freezing, especially cassia, cardamoms and cloves as they tend to become a bit astringent.

5. Get the dish into the freezer as soon as it is cold. Do not freeze if the food has been kept warm for a long time or reheated, especially chicken. There is a risk of bacterial contamination.

6. Be aware that spicy food can 'taint' other foods, so preferably pack in a plastic container with an airtight lid.

7. Label with contents and freeze date, and use within 3 months.

8. When reheating ensure that the dish is thoroughly hot and cooked through.

9. You may find the spicing has gone a little bland, so taste and cook in more spices as needed.

10. Finally, *never ever* freeze, thaw and refreeze an item.

CONSISTENCY OF BALTI DISHES

The ideal consistency of Balti is a dryish to creamy texture, depending on your preference. Water or stock can be added during the simmering if it is too dry. Alternatively, if too wet, keep simmering until it reaches the desired consistency.

BALTI MEALS

Portions

Appetites vary enormously, and one person's 'huge' plateful may leave a neighbour hungry.

When I entertain or supply food for paying customers, I always provide enormous helpings. It is far better to have fully satisfied diners, than the other way round. You know the signs of the still-hungry diner: the available food disappears fast, very fast, then the diner looks furtively around, whites of the eyes indicating the preliminary signs of panic. Some restaurants, it seems, are unable to learn the signs. I've seen portions so skimpy that an anorexic teenager would pass out, rice layered so thinly on the salver, that you can see more salver than rice. So serve generously and enjoy your diners' enjoyment. I can live with 'should-never-have-eaten-so-much' complaints. They're not meant in any case.

So what is a generous portion? My average serving per person is 6 oz (175 g) nett weight of the principal ingredient before cooking (i.e., after being divested of anything inedible). The average Balti dish will include a further 2 oz (50 g) of flavouring and thickening ingredients (spices, garlic, ginger, onion, tomatoes, pepper etc). All dishes say how many portions they make.

A Balti meal is fun with a number of main dishes. The more people who are eating the meal, the easier this is. With four people you might serve one meat, one poultry, one fish or shellfish, and two vegetable Balti dishes, plus rice, bread and chutneys. Allow approximately 2 oz (50 g) (uncooked weight) of each of the five dishes for each person, plus 2–3 oz (50–75 g) extra. For rice allow 2 oz (50 g) dry uncooked weight per person for a small portion, 3 oz (75 g) for larger appetites. For lentils, allow 1 oz (25 g) uncooked weight, minimum, per person.

If all this sounds complicated it isn't really. As always, common sense should prevail.

As much of the enjoyment of Balti eating is to mix-and-match combinations of items (see below), I have adopted a portions formula in this book which should help you. All meat, chicken and fish or shellfish recipes are given as four-portion servings. Vegetables, on the other hand are given as single-portion servings. Some items which you may wish to use a lot of – par-cooked meat, lentils, etc – are also given in 'bulk' ten-portion recipes. Using some fresh and some frozen, this will save you time, smells and multiple washing up.

Balti Combination Dishes

The majority of recipes in this book are complete in themselves and can be served as they are, with some rice and/or bread.

For the adventurous, however, the fun has only just begun! The beauty of Balti is that the dishes are designed to be combined in any way that takes your fancy or suits the contents of your fridge or freezer. This can be as simple as adding some plain vegetables to a particular Balti dish, or could involve combining two, three or more given Balti dishes into one spectacular combination Balti dish.

There are no rules. The only thing to remember is that you should aim to have 4 portions of main ingredients per dish to serve

4 people. The main ingredients can be meat, poultry, fish or shellfish, vegetables or paneer (Indian cheese).

So for example, if you decided to combine Balti Turkey Curry with some celery (or indeed any other vegetable from Chapter 5), for every 1 portion of cooked celery (6 oz/175 g raw weight) added to the recipe on page 72, you would reduce the amount of raw turkey by the same amount.

Similarly, if you wanted to combine Balti Prawns (page 86) with Balti Keema (56), you would need only half quantity of each recipe (since both recipes make 4 portions), to serve 4 people.

For tips and suggestions on combining actual Balti dishes, see Chapter 7.

Serving

Traditionally, the various dishes should come to the table in a blackened, well-used Balti pot – the two-handled, wok-like pan described on page 15. A smarter alternative is a chromium-plated version. These dishes come in a variety of sizes.

For preference, at home, I like to issue the diner with a Balti pan to eat out of, the ideal size being 10–11 in (25–27.5cm) in diameter. The food itself can be served in similar-sized pans or smaller versions of around 5 in (12.5cm) in diameter for individual portions. Put these on dinner plates and/or side plates. Willow pattern is favourite at the Balti house, but any type will do.

Bread can be served in a huge Balti pan of around 14 in (35cm) in diameter, whilst chutneys look great in tiny ones of around 3 in (7.5cm). (See page 17 for advice regarding the obtaining of these items.)

As for eating Balti, the traditional way in the Balti lands and at the Balti house is to use no cutlery. The *chupatti* or *naan* is the traditional 'implement'. Break off a smallish wedge and using your right hand only, scoop up the food with the bread and pop it and the bread into your mouth. After practice it becomes quite easy and not at all messy. Leave enough bread to do the traditional wipe-up of the dish at the end. For the faint-hearted, a fork and dessertspoon are the only acceptable cutlery. A finger bowl and ample napkins are mandatory. And plenty of finger lickin' is expected of you!

Alcohol and Beverages

Balti comes from a strict Moslem country. Alcohol is not consumed there, although the rules are bent a little for foreign tourists. In the same vein, whilst some Balti houses have become licensed, most allow patrons to bring their own drink in at no charge. In this way they do not profit from the sale of alcohol, so they accord with the rules of the Koran.

The traditional beverages to accompany Balti are water, fruit juices, cordials (one of the most popular being freshly squeezed lemon or lime juice with ice and water), and *lhassi* (yoghurt with water, crushed ice, spices and salt or sugar).

For non-Moslems, beers (notably lager) are still the most popular drink, with over 55 per cent of diners preferring it. One of the very best is Cobra lager, manufactured in India, and specifically brewed for spicy foods.

Some robust dry red, white and rosé wines also go well with Balti cooking. Sparkling whites or rosés and of course, champagne, cannot be beaten. There are no rules and the choice is yours.

BASIC INGREDIENTS

Items as dissimilar as coconut, cooking oil and coriander leaves are as important as garlic, ginger and ghee in Balti cooking. They and other important items appear on the next few pages. Appendix 2 on page 149 gives a list of other ingredients you'll need in your store cupboard and without which it is impossible to proceed.

Oils and Fats

Edible oil and fat can be produced from many vegetables and nuts and from meat, fish, poultry, etc. It can also be produced from milk in the form of butter.

Balti cooking depends very greatly on the use of oil to establish both taste and texture, particularly in the early stages of cooking. And there is no argument that using *more* oil creates a better curry than using less. There is a limit to this, of course. We are all probably familiar with curries swimming in oil served in some restaurants. In such a case, too much oil was used in the first place, and no matter how good the end result, the excess oil spoils the dish. It could so easily have been spooned off at the end of its

cooking while still in its saucepan. Once a properly cooked Balti is taken off direct heat and allowed to rest, all the oil rises to the top and can then be ladled off for future use in curry cooking.

In this country we can get many suitable oils. For deep-frying I use a good quality odourless corn oil. This will do for all your cookery actually. A light oil – sunflower oil, for example – is superb for lightly stir-fried vegetable dishes. It is odourless and is ideal in that it does not affect delicate and subtle dishes.

These days nutritionists are aware of health risks concerning certain fats and oils. Solid fats are described as saturated and can lead to a build-up of cholesterol in the body. Saturated fats include rendered animal fat such as dripping and lard. Butter, clarified butter and butter ghee come into this category and, to a lesser extent, solid margarine and vegetable ghee. Ghee (pronounced with a hard G as in geese) is widely used in the cooking of Baltistan and Kashmir, and is clarified butter or margarine. It is expensive to buy but easy to make. Oils described as polyunsaturated are said to be better, and these include certain vegetable oils such as sunflower and soya oil. Best of all are said to be monounsaturated oils which include peanut and mustard oils, both excellent for curry cooking. One oil you should *never* use in any Balti cooking, however, is olive oil. It imparts a strong flavour which does not go at all well with Balti cuisine.

In many dishes the oil used affects the final taste very minimally, so most oils can be used instead of ghee. But in rice and bread cooking, ghee imparts an important flavour. I have tried to strike a happy balance in these recipes by specifying neither too much nor too little ghee or oil. You can always use more if that is to your taste, and remember to spoon off excess before serving.

Facing page 24: Balti Sag Gosht (page 49) with added red pepper (page 98), served with Balti Naan (pages 144–5)

Opposite: Balti Chicken Tikka Masala (page 67), served with Plain Boiled Rice (page 138)

GHEE

Ghee is a clarified butter, is very easy to make and gives a distinctive and delicious taste. When cooled and set, it will keep for several months without refrigeration.

If you want to make vegetable ghee, simply use pure vegetable block margarine instead of butter.

2 lb (900 g) any butter

1 Place the butter blocks whole into a medium non-stick pan. Melt at a very low heat.

2 When completely melted, raise heat very slightly. Ensure it does not smoke or burn, but don't stir. Leave to cook for about 1 hour. The impurities will sink to the bottom and float on the top. Carefully skim any off the top with a slotted spoon, but don't touch the bottom.

3 Turn off the heat and allow the ghee to cool a little. Then strain it through kitchen paper or muslin into an airtight storage jar. When it cools it solidifies, although it is quite soft. It should be a bright pale lemon colour and it smells like toffee. If it has burned it will be darker and smell different. Providing it is not too burned it can still be used.

Coconut

Coconut is not native to Baltistan – the region is too cold for it to grow – but as a flavouring, it is an excellent additive. Fresh is best, but coconuts are fiddly to open and you are left with a lot of flesh (which can be frozen of course).

Desiccated coconut is one substitute for fresh coconut, and can be used by adding it dry to your cooking, or by simmering it in water and straining it to create coconut milk. Canned coconut milk is much richer and thicker and a good product is coconut milk powder – very finely ground, dried, coconut flesh – which has a creamier taste than desiccated, and mixes well with water.

The Curry Club makes the familiar 7 oz (200 g) rich block of **creamed coconut** which is a combination of freshly grated coconut flesh and coconut oil, which sets solid. It must be kept under refrigeration. To use, boil a little water. Cut off the amount required and melt it in the hot water. If you try to fry it without water, it will burn.

Flour

In many parts of the Indian sub-continent, including Baltistan, wheat is the staple food, not rice. The basic flours used for Indian breads are wholemeal flour (the Indian version is called ata flour or chupatti flour and is available from Asian suppliers or The Curry Club), self-raising flour and strong plain white flour. Ata flour is made from hard wheat and is more finely ground than our flour. This combination makes it more glutinous.

Garlic

Garlic is indispensable to Balti cooking. It is best to buy one or more bulbs on which are clustered a number of individual cloves. The skin is discarded and you should be left with a creamy, plump firm clove. To use, I prefer to chop the cloves finely (you can use a spring vegetable chopper), but you can use a garlic crusher (I think these are messy to clean, and wasteful). You can also simply crush them under the flat side of a knife blade. To purée garlic, use an electric food processor or mortar and pestle.

Ginger

Ginger is a rhizome or root which grows underground, and is native to Asia and other suitable climates. It comes in three forms – fresh, whole dried, and as powder. Fresh is the best way, and it stays fresh for many months after being cropped.

Ginger is readily available at UK greengrocers. Size is not always a guide to quality. It should look plump, not withered, and have a pinky beige skin and a slight sheen. When cut the ginger should be a primrose-cream colour with no sign at all of blue or staleness. It is not possible to tell if it is stale until you cut it, so if you know your greengrocer well, ask him to cut it before you buy it. It should not be stringy or very dry and tough.

To use ginger you must first cut off any 'scars' but it is not necessary to peel it.

Onion

Probably, second to spices, the most important ingredient in Balti cooking is onion. It provides a savoury flavour, and it is also important for thickening sauces.

The best onions to use for Balti cooking are the mild Spanish ones. On average they weigh around 8 oz (225 g) each, and are easy to peel and prepare.

FRIED DEHYDRATED ONION FLAKES
— ♦ —

Several recipes call for fried dehydrated onion flakes as an ingredient or a garnish. It's a good idea to make a batch and store in an airtight tin (they will keep for several weeks).

8 tablespoons sunflower oil   *6 oz (175 g) bought dehydrated onion flakes*

1 Heat the oil, then add the onion flakes.
2 Briskly stir-fry for around 1 minute. (They will burn easily so keep them moving.)
3 Remove from the heat and drain.

Coriander

The main herb used in Balti cooking is fresh coriander leaf which has a very distinctive, acquired, musky taste, a little redolent of the not unpleasant fragrance of candle wax. But it is very important, and contributes greatly to achieving authentic flavours. The leaves only are used; the stalks are a little bitter and are discarded (although guinea pigs and rabbits adore them, so if you or your friends or their kids ...).

Fresh parsley can be substituted if you can't get coriander, which does not taste the same, but *looks* nice. Gardeners will probably be able to grow coriander but things like that are above and beyond me.

When purchasing fresh coriander, the problems are twofold.

Firstly, although it is flown in fresh from Cyprus, Egypt and Greece daily, and it is also grown in the UK, some greengrocers stubbornly refuse to stock it. If you have some of those in your town, go to your local curry house and ask which greengrocer supplies them. Whoever it is will supply coriander. Second, although it is not expensive, coriander comes in great big bunches. A lot can be wasted if it's not used within a day or so. (Keep it in water, and change this daily: this will prolong its life.) A bunch will yield an average of 2–2½ oz (50–70 g), or 4–5 tablespoons of chopped leaf and light stalks.

To preserve it, simply chop fresh coriander, dry it if necessary on kitchen paper, and freeze by itself. You can also freeze it chopped, in ice cubes, for adding to curries prior to serving.

USING SPICES

Storing Spices

Whole spices retain their flavour longer than ground, for one year or more sometimes. Ground spices give off a stronger aroma than whole, and of course this means their storage life is that much shorter. Three months is about right for most ground items. So plan your larder accordingly, and buy little and often and grind freshly. Keep the spices out of sunlight (better in a dark cupboard), and in airtight labelled containers. Clean coffee or jam jars are excellent.

Grinding Spices

It is better by far to grind your own whole spices whenever you can. Firstly you can be sure of the quality and contents, and secondly they will be fresher and tastier. The traditional method is by mortar and pestle, but you can use an electric coffee grinder or the new electric spice mill (see page 18). Use small quantities to prevent overloading the motor.

Don't try to grind dry ginger or turmeric. They are too fibrous for most small grinders, and commercial powders are adequate. Peppers – chilli, paprika and black or white pepper – are tricky to grind yourself and commercially ground powders will suffice. The oilier spices such as cloves, nutmeg, brown cardamoms and bay leaves are easier to grind if roasted first.

In the recipes, when a spice is referred to as 'ground', this means factory ground. Where it requires the spice to be home-ground (usually after roasting), the recipe clearly states this.

Cooking Whole Spices

Whole spices contain essential or volatile oils. It is these which we can smell when handling a spice, and it is these which we must release when we cook with spices.

Roasting

Roasting whole spices is my favourite way of releasing their essential oils. A roasted whole spice tastes quite different from a raw one and the release of flavour is pleasantly overwhelming. Some recipes specify roasting of the spices.

The roasting process is simple and can be done in a dry pan on the stove, in a dry electric frying pan, under the grill or in the oven. Each spice should be heated until it gives off its aroma. The heat should be medium rather than hot and the time required is a few minutes. (Preheat the oven to 325°F/160°C/Gas 3 and allow about 10 minutes.) The spice should not blacken; a light brown at most is sufficient. The original oil of the spice must not be totally cooked out or it will lose its flavour. A little experimenting will soon show you how to do it. In some recipes pre-roasted spices are important. (Incidentally, coffee is roasted in exactly the same manner as spices.)

Frying

Some of the recipes in this book require you to *fry* whole spices. The process is known as the *bargar*, and is done for the same reason as the roasting of whole spices – to cook out the raw taste from the spices and release the aromatic oils. The oil should be hot, and the spices are put straight into the oil. You must use your judgement as to when they are cooked. Do not let them blacken. As soon as they begin to change colour or to float they are ready. It will not take more than a couple of minutes.

If you burn the spices during this bargar process *you must throw the result away and start again*. Better to waste a small amount of spices than taint a whole meal.

Blending Spices

This sounds rather grandiose. In fact it's simple. Every mixture is called a blend. Generally we mean ground spices, and of course the best-known blends of all (with the worst reputation) are curry powders. Many of my recipes use blends of two or more ground spices. So in effect we make our own 'curry powder' every time we use one of these recipes. 'Curry powder' gives a totally wrong image and is generally despised by cooks in all the curry lands, who call any mixture of spices the '*masala*'.

Each recipe has its own masala and it is this unique combination of spices which makes Balti-style cooking so distinctive. The following curry powder recipe is a masala, but throughout the ingredients lists in my recipes I refer to the masala as 'spices' (whole or ground).

BALTI MASALA MIX
— ♦ —

You can use commercial curry powder to create a Balti base, but long though the spice list is, it is easy to produce your own, and far better. Firstly it is formulated by yourself so, obvious though this sounds, you know exactly what is in it. Unlike some factory-made powder, you will have no stalks, no rubbish and no poor-quality spices. Secondly, you can vary the formula to suit your taste. Thirdly, no factory roasts spices, so yours will taste infinitely superior.

As soon as your masala mix is made, store it in an airtight, damp-free container away from the light (the ultra violet in daylight 'fades' both the colour and the taste). It is better left to 'mature' for about a month. It should then be used sooner rather than later. It will be at its best within six months. After that it will gradually lose its subtle flavours and become bitter.

The amount of masala you use depends on your taste. For a spicy dish you may use 8 g or about 2 level teaspoons per portion. For a mild dish it may be as little as 4 g or about 1 level teaspoon per portion. Thus 200 g (7 oz) will yield as few as 25 single-portion servings and as many as 50. You can scale the quantities up or down in the exact proportions to make a larger or smaller quantity of this masala.

Please note that spices vary in density from species to species and batch to batch, depending largely on moisture content, so obtaining 100 per cent accuracy is unlikely. The 'accurate' gram column is for guidance only. In any case, you can adjust quantities of favourite spices to your own taste. I've used metric measures only because it is easier to be accurate with small measures.

Spoon measures here are heaped.

Makes about 7 oz (200 g)

WHOLE SPICES

50 g (4 tablespoons) coriander seeds
30 g (2 tablespoons) white cummin seeds
15 g (3 x 2 in/5 cm) pieces cassia bark
10 g (2 teaspoons) fennel seeds
10 g (2 teaspoons) black mustard seeds
8 g (2 teaspoons) green cardamom seeds
4 g (1 teaspoon) fenugreek seeds
4 g (1 teaspoon) lovage seeds
3 g (½ teaspoon) wild onion seeds

3 g (6–8) cloves
2 g (1 tablespoon) dry fenugreek leaves
2 g (4–6) bay leaves
2 g (20–25) dry curry leaves

GROUND SPICES

20 g (4 teaspoons) turmeric
20 g (4 teaspoons) garlic powder
10 g (2 teaspoons) ginger powder
8 g (1½ teaspoons) chilli powder

1 Roast, cool and grind the whole spices.

2 Mix well with the ground spices and store.

BALTI GARAM MASALA

— ♦ —

Garam masala is one of the keys to North Indian, Moghul and Pakistani and Balti cooking. Literally meaning hot (*garam*) mixture of spices (*masala*), it is used to perk up dishes towards the end of their cooking.

There are as many recipes for garam masala as there are cooks and, as with the previous recipe, you will probably wish to vary the ingredients to suit your taste. This is an authentic Kashmiri garam masala where the emphasis is on aromatics rather than heat. Again I've used approximate measures (spoons) and more accurate measures in metric only. Spoons are heaped.

Makes about 7 oz (200 g)

60 g (4¹/₂ tablespoons) coriander seeds
40 g (2¹/₂ tablespoons) white cummin seeds
25 g (5 teaspoons) aniseed
25 g (5 x 2 in/5 cm) pieces cassia bark
25 g (1¹/₂ tablespoons) green cardamom seeds

15 g (1 tablespoon) cloves
5 g (1¹/₂ teaspoons) dried mint leaves
2 g (4–6) bay leaves
2 g (1 tablespoon) dry rose petals (optional)
¹/₂ g (1 teaspoon) saffron stamens (optional)

1 Lightly roast everything under a low to medium grill or in a low oven. Do not let the spices burn. They should give off a light steam.

2 When they give off an aroma remove from the heat, cool and grind in batches.

3 After grinding, mix thoroughly and store in an airtight jar. Garam masala will last almost indefinitely, but it is always better to make small fresh batches every few months to get the best flavours.

AROMATIC SALT
— ♦ —

Throughout this book, recipes call for aromatic salt. This is salt, preferably sea salt, to which is added a light spice mixture. Ordinary salt can be used in its place, but the spicing adds a delicacy and subtlety to a recipe. It is a trick I picked up from professional chefs, and I highly recommend it.

Here are two recipes, the first being light and aromatic, the second containing spicier tastes as well as nuts. Finely grind a reasonably-sized batch of your preferred aromatic salt and store in a screw-top jar.

1
LIGHTLY SPICED AROMATIC SALT
100 g (4 oz) coarsely granulated sea salt
1 teaspoon cinnamon
1 teaspoon ground allspice

2
SPICIER AROMATIC SALT
1 quantity lightly spiced salt
$^1/_2$ teaspoon ground fenugreek seeds
1 teaspoon dried mint
1 tablespoon ground almond
$^1/_2$ teaspoon turmeric

PANCH PHORAN
— ♦ —

This is a Bengali mixture of five (*panch*) spices. There are several possible combinations, but this is my favourite.

Simply mix together equal parts of (a teaspoon of each is plenty):

white cummin seeds
fennel seeds
fenugreek seeds

mustard seeds
wild onion seeds

TANDOORI DRY MIX MASALA

As with all pre-mixed masalas, this has the advantage of maturing during storage. Keep it in the dark in an airtight container, and it will be good for about 12 months.

The bright reds and oranges that we associate with restaurant tandooris and tikkas are phoney, requiring chemical colourings. Instead I use beetroot powder and anatto seed powder, which produce less vibrant colour. If you want the artificial restaurant look, use 5 g red and 3 g sunset yellow food colouring instead. All spoon measures are heaped.

Makes about 7 oz (200 g)

30 g (2 tablespoons) ground coriander
25 g (5 teaspoons) ground cummin
25 g (5 teaspoons) garlic powder
25 g (5 teaspoons) paprika
20 g (4 teaspoons) mango powder

20 g (6 teaspoons) dried mint
20 g (4 teaspoons) beetroot powder (deep red colouring)
15 g (3 teaspoons) chilli powder
10 g (2 teaspoons) anatto seed powder (yellow colouring)
10 g (2 teaspoons) aromatic salt (see previous recipe)

1 Simply mix the ingredients together well, and store.

2 Use as described in the recipes.

Cooking Ground Spices

Whole spices need to be roasted or fried to bring out their aromas (see page 30). It is less obvious that ground spices must be cooked too. In fact it is even more important. Factory-ground spices are never pre-roasted so they have 'raw' tastes. Anyone who has had the misfortune to experience the old-style British canteen curry will know what this means. Curry powder is spooned straight into a bubbling stew. The result is appalling, and has single-handedly set back this nation's appreciation of curry by decades.

It is easy to cook ground spices. They simply have to be fried. Some cooks just add powdered spices to hot oil. But it is all too easy to burn the spices this way. The most reliable way to cook ground spices is to make the dry masala into a wet paste by adding water.

Making a Masala Paste

1 Place the masala in a mixing bowl large enough to enable you to stir it, and do so until it is fully mixed.

2 Add enough water to form a stiff paste *and no more*. (Vinegar is used in some masala pastes to help preserve them.)

3 Leave to stand for a minimum of 10 minutes. It does not matter how long it stands. This ensures that the ground spices absorb all the water.

4 Add a little water if it is too dry prior to using in the bhoona or frying process.

Recipes for masala pastes appear on pages 38–9.

The Bhoona (Frying a Masala Paste)
Bhoona is the term for the process of cooking a masala paste in hot oil. This is an important part of the curry-cooking process which removes the raw taste of the spices, and influences the final taste of the dish.

Traditionally you should fry the spice paste first, then add the chopped onion second. This method can easily cause burned spices so I reverse the process and have found that it works very satisfactorily. Instructions are given in the recipes, but here is a more detailed description of the process.

1. Take a round-sided pan such as a Balti pan, karahi or wok. If you don't have one, use an ordinary frying pan (a non-stick one is best).

2. Heat the oil to quite a high heat (but not smoking). Fry the garlic (and whole spices if required) briskly for a few minutes. Then reduce the heat, add the onions, and commence stirring.

3. *From this point do not let your attention wander.* Keep stirring the onion and gently add the masala paste (and, in most of the recipes in this book, the main ingredient). Beware of splattering, but keep stirring. The water in the paste lowers the temperature. Do not let the mixture stick at all. Do not stop stirring, not even for a few seconds.

4. After a few minutes the water will have evaporated out and the oil will float above the mixture. The spices will be cooked.

Curry Pastes, Gravy and Stock

Anyone interested in Indian food must have encountered bottled curry or masala pastes on the grocery shelves. There are many makes and types, but little explanation as to what they are or what they do. They are designed to take the labour out of blending a spice mixture, making it into a water paste and frying it. The manufacturers do it all for you, adding vinegar (acetic acid) and hot oil to prevent it from going mouldy. Unfortunately they also add salt and chilli powder which make the pastes a little overpowering. They are very concentrated, and you only need a small quantity for cooking.

These bought curry pastes are already cooked, but to 'disguise' them you will probably need to add some other whole or ground spices, and you will certainly need to fry garlic, ginger, onion, etc. Simply add the spice paste after these three are fried and carry on with the rest of the recipe.

It's much better to make your own, and here are a few recipes:

BALTI MASALA PASTE

— ◆ —

This mild paste forms the base for most Balti dishes. Using vinegar (rather than all water) to make the paste will enable you to preserve it in jars. As with all pickling, sterilise the jars (a good hot wash followed by a dry-out in a low-heat oven will do). Top off the paste in the jar with hot oil and inspect after a few days to see that there is no mould.

Makes about 1¹/₂ lb (675 g)

1 recipe Balti masala mix (see page 31)
6–8 fl oz (175–250 ml) vinegar (any type)

6–8 fl oz (175–250 ml) vegetable oil

1 Place the ground masala spices in a bowl.

2 Add the vinegar and enough water to make a creamy paste. Leave to stand for at least 10 minutes.

3 Heat the oil in a karahi or wok.

4 Add the paste to the oil. It will splatter a bit so be careful.

5 Stir-fry the paste continually to prevent it sticking until the water content is cooked out (it should take about 5 minutes). As the liquid is reduced, the paste will begin to make a regular bubbling noise (hard to describe, but it goes chup-chup-chup-chup) if you don't stir, and it will splatter. This is your audible cue that it is ready.

   You can tell if the spices are cooked by taking the karahi off the stove. Leave to stand for 3–4 minutes. If the oil 'floats' to the top, the spices are cooked. If not, add a little more oil and carry on cooking and stirring.

6 Bottle the paste in sterilised jars. Then heat up a little more oil and 'cap' off the paste by pouring in enough oil to cover. Seal the jars and store.

GREEN MASALA PASTE

— ♦ —

This curry paste is green in colour because of its use of coriander and mint. You can buy it factory made, but it does not have the delicious fresh taste of this recipe from Ivan Watson, journalist and regular correspondent to *The Curry Magazine*.

Makes about 1 lb (450 g)

1 teaspoon fenugreek seeds
6 garlic cloves, chopped
2 tablespoons finely chopped
    fresh ginger
1½ oz (40 g) fresh mint leaves
1½ oz (40 g) fresh coriander
    leaves
4 fl oz (120 ml) vinegar

3 teaspoons salt
3 teaspoons turmeric
2 teaspoons chilli powder
½ teaspoon ground cloves
1 teaspoon ground cardamom
    seeds
4 fl oz (120 ml) vegetable oil
2 fl oz (50 ml) sesame oil

1 Soak the fenugreek seeds in water overnight. They will swell and acquire a jelly-like coating.

2 Strain the fenugreek, discarding the water.

3 Mulch down all the ingredients, except the oils, in a blender or food processor, to make a purée. Leave to stand for at least 10 minutes.

4 Heat the oil in a karahi or wok and follow stages 4–6 of the previous recipe.

TANDOORI MASALA PASTE

— ♦ —

Most restaurants use bright red tandoori paste to colour and spice their marinades. It is not difficult to make your own.

Follow the recipe for Balti masala paste (on page 38), substituting 1 recipe of the tandoori dry mix masala (on page 35) for the Balti masala mix.

CHAPTER 2

Meat

The animals which have been associated with civilised mankind longer than any others are sheep and goats. Their domestication goes back to around 10,000 BC and they pre-date domesticated cattle and pigs by thousands of years. It is still goat and mutton which, for historical reasons, remain the most prevalent meat amongst the Moslem population of today's Balti lands.

Young goat (kid) and young sheep (lamb) are rarely eaten there day to day as they are considered to be a luxury. It is far better, they believe, to let the animal reach maturity. Because of this their meat requires long slow cooking to tenderise it. In the English-speaking lands, however, we prefer the milder flavour of lamb, and we breed our animals so that they reach their peak of yield and flavour at under one year old. The long slow cooking of Balti as carried out in Baltistan is not necessary if we take advantage of the good quality cuts of meat available to us.

In the West we also have the benefit of an unrestricted choice of lamb, mutton, veal, beef, pork, kid, goat, venison and other furred game, and their offal.

LAMB AND MUTTON

Lamb is a young sheep under a year old, when its carcass weighs about 40 lb (18 kg). The largest lamb carcass weighs about 55 lb (25 kg), while a mutton carcass weighs up to 90 lb (40 kg).

The best cuts of lamb are the leanest which, inevitably, are also the most expensive. Leg is the best joint, and the very best, most expensive lamb cut is called leg steak. This comes from the top of the leg and can be supplied boneless.

You can ask for diced lamb stewing steak quality, cut from any combination of meat, or kebab quality cut only from leg. The former will be more fatty, but less expensive; it will also take longer to cook to tenderness.

KID AND GOAT

Kid is a young goat under a year old, and both kid and goat meat are available only from specialist butchers.

The meat is tougher than mutton, and the carcass is smaller. It has a stronger flavour, but in other respects the cuts of meat are much the same as those described for lamb and mutton.

BEEF AND VEAL

Cattle have been domesticated since about 6,000 BC. In the sub-continent, the Moslems are not averse to it, but Hindus will not eat beef or veal, and the cow is venerated to such an extent that it wanders at will across main roads, railways and markets. I well remember seeing an aged beast standing next to a vegetable stall near Mysore, swishing its tail across the adjoining knick-knack stall. Whilst both the stall-holders were preoccupied with damage limitation at the rear end, the front end was chomping away at assorted fruit and vegetables. When the vegetable stall-holder finally cottoned on, the beast was shooed away. But woe betide anyone who hurts or kills a cow.

A beef carcass weighs up to 800 lb (360 kg). The boned roasting cuts come from the leg – topside, top rump and silverside. The rear top back of the carcass provides the tenderest meat in the form of boned steaks – rump, loin, and sirloin. Tenderest of all is the long fillet, cut from under the sirloin. Ask the butcher to supply it 'larder trimmed' if you want all unwanted matter removed. It will then weigh between $3^{1}/_{2}$–5 lb (1.5–2.3 kg).

A cheaper cut is chuck steak, which is available butcher diced, and with no more than 20 per cent fat permitted or, cheaper still, pie meat (diced), also called stewing steak, in which 25 per cent fat is permitted. Both these cuts come from the front end of the carcass, and will need longer, slower cooking than prime cuts.

PORK

The wild pig evolved in the Orient and was the only animal to be domesticated by the Ancient Chinese, at least by 6,000 BC. It is still the most important meat in the Far East. It is aso popular in Europe, America and Australia. The consumption of pork is forbidden by Moslems and Jews for religious reasons.

Pig is rarely eaten before it reaches 9 months old, the only exception being suckling pig (which should be no more than 8 weeks old).

The leanest and tenderest meat comes from the leg – silverside boned joint meat, leg steaks and escalopes, for instance. Fillet tender loin steaks are also cut from boneless middle (hogmeat). Diced stewing pork is relatively cheap, but requires longer cooking.

OFFAL

Offal is the off-cuts or 'off fall' of parts from meat carcasses. Heart, liver and kidney are the most popular offal ingredients. Other items include tongue, brains, lung (lights), spleen (milt), pancreas (sweetbreads), feet (trotters) and tail (ox). The stomach (tripe) is from cattle only.

Offal is ideal for stir-frying and it goes well with Balti spices. It can be substituted for, or used with meat in any of the recipes in this chapter. See Chef's Tip 2 on page 47.

GAME

The term game used to apply only to wild animals and birds that were hunted. Most game today is bred specifically for eating.

Game is divided into two categories – non-flighted and flighted, or furred and feathered. In this chapter we briefly look at non-flighted game. Chapter 3 deals with flighted game.

Venison

Venison is the meat of deer up to $2^{1}/_{2}$ years in age, which are specially bred for the table. Fresh venison is seasonal, but the freezer makes it available all year round. Venison must be hung by the butcher to maximise tenderness and flavour. It is ideal for marination and spicy applications, and curries extremely well.

The meat is dark red and, as with most meat, the best cuts are the haunch and saddle (rear leg and top back). Cheaper cuts come from the loin, shoulder and neck. With venison more than other meats it is advisable to remove all fat because its taste after cooking is quite bitter.

Cooking times will vary depending on the type of venison and the cut, but in general are those of lamb.

Wild Boar

The ancestor of the domestic pig, wild boar once thrived in England's forests, but has long since been hunted out of existence. In Europe, France and Germany in particular, and in India, it still prevails and is very popular.

Young wild boar around 6 months old (called marcassin) is very tender, but normally the animal must be between a year and four years old to be suitable for the table. Cuts of meat are as for pork, but wild boar is leaner than domesticated pigs.

Rabbit

There are two types of rabbit available, wild or domesticated. The meat of the wild animal is darker and stronger in flavour.

Rabbit carcasses should be skinned just prior to use and can weigh from $2^{1}/_{2}$-20 lb (1.1 kg-9 kg). Best in flavour are 4-month rabbits weighing around 5 lb (2.25 kg). The meat yield will be no more than one-quarter of the carcass weight, so buy whole or jointed into legs and back pieces, fresh or frozen.

Hare

Hare flesh is darker, and its taste is gamier than rabbit. A 1-year hare weighs $5^{1}/_{2}$-$6^{1}/_{2}$ lb (2.5–3 kg) and older animals weigh up to 13 lb (6 kg). The yearling is considered best for flavour and will yield enough meat for two to four servings, cooked on the bone (roughly 15–20 minutes per pound/450 g).

MEAT COOKING TIMES

The timings required to cook different meats for Balti curries vary from meat to meat. Beef seems to take less time than lamb, for example. And different cuts of beef will require different times, depending on quality, as already mentioned: the tenderest, most expensive fillet will cook quicker than pie meat. The size of the cube will also affect timings. The smaller the cube the quicker the cooking. It is therefore impossible to give precise cooking times for meat, as there are so many variables. Follow the guidelines in the recipes and test for tenderness where instructed in the method.

Whatever meat you use in Balti cooking, however, it must be well cooked. It must be as tender as you can get it without it breaking up into a stringy mush. So the times I give must be regarded as average. Test by tasting, and keep cooking until you are happy with the tenderness.

Cooking Meat on the Bone

Meat will almost always be cooked 'on the bone' in the Balti area of Pakistan. If you wish to cook it like this, get the butcher to cut the meat on the bone into quite small pieces. After removing fat and gristle you should obtain a net weight of 8 lb (3.6 kg) lean meat on the bone to make 16 portions. Extend the par-cooking time (see next recipe) by 10–15 minutes and test for tenderness.

BALTI MEAT COOKING METHODS

Most people from the Balti lands are devout meat eaters. The original traditional Balti cooking methods involve hours of very slow cooking over charcoal embers, enabling the meat to become slowly infused with the flavours of the spices and to become tender perfection. Undeniably this method achieves exceptionally good results, but most of us will not have dying embers to hand, nor several hours to spend watching the pot.

Instead the recipes in this chapter all require par-cooked meat, and the instructions for par-cooking are opposite. If you intend to make a lot of Balti meat curries, I recommend part cooking of a large quantity of meat which you can divide up into containers and cool and freeze.

PAR-COOKED BALTI LAMB
— ◆ —

Par-cooked meat forms the basis of all the recipes in this chapter, so I have given sufficient quantities below to produce enough par-cooked meat to make four Balti recipes.

I have specified lamb here, but you could use any type of meat (see Chef's Tip below).

Makes enough for 16 portions

6 lb (2.7 kg) lamb steak, cut into ¼ inch (32 mm) cubes, and weighed after discarding unwanted matter

1 pint (600 ml) stock or water
4 tablespoons Balti masala paste (see page 38)

1 Using a large lidded casserole dish, bring the stock or water to the boil. Add the meat and the paste and bring to the simmer, stirring as needed.

2 Put the lidded dish into the oven, pre-heated to 375°F/190°C/Gas 5.

3 Cook for 20 minutes. Inspect and stir adding a little water if needed. Cook for 20 more minutes. Test for tenderness: it should still have a bite, and not be quite ready. If not yet at this stage, continue cooking a while longer.

4 When it is at this stage, remove it from the casserole, strain and reserve the liquid. Cool down the meat, divide into containers and freeze.

5 Alternatively, some or all of the par cooked meat can be used to carry on with the Balti meat recipes.

6 The stock can be used to create a tasty curry sauce.

CHEF'S TIP

Cubed beef may require a little less time, veal almost certainly will. Mutton and goat will require a little more time, as will venison and pork.

Pieces of meat on the bone will require more time too – see page 44.

BALTI MEAT, MEDIUM HEAT

— ◆ —

This is a 'standard' medium-heat Balti preparation. It should result in tender bite-sized cubes of meat in an ample golden brown, pleasantly flavoured, spicy curry gravy, neither too hot, nor too mild.

Serves 4 *(makes 4 portions)*

4 portions par-cooked Balti
  meat (see page 45)

2–3 tablespoons ghee or corn oil
3–6 garlic cloves, finely
  chopped
8 oz (225 g) onion, very finely
  chopped
3–4 tablespoons Balti masala
  paste (see page 38)

about 7 fl oz (200 ml) reserved
  stock (see page 45), Balti
  chicken stock (see page 65) or
  water
1 tablespoon Balti garam
  masala (see page 33)
1 tablespoon very finely
  chopped fresh coriander
  leaves
aromatic salt to taste (see page
  34)

1 Heat the ghee or oil in your karahi on high heat, then stir-fry the garlic for 30 seconds.

2 Add the onion on a reduced heat, and stir-fry for about 10 minutes, allowing the onion to become translucent and begin to brown.

3 Add the masala paste and the par-cooked meat. Raise the heat again and bring to a brisk sizzle, stir-frying as needed for about 5 minutes.

4 Add the reserved stock or water bit by bit and simmer, stirring, on a lower heat for about 10 minutes.

5 Test for tenderness. If more cooking is needed add stock or water as required. When as you like it, add the garam masala, fresh coriander leaves and aromatic salt to taste.

6 Simmer for 15 minutes more, then serve.

CHEF'S TIP 1

If you do not have any Balti masala paste made up you can use any bottled curry paste as a substitute, although the results will not be as good.

Alternatively use 3–4 tablespoons Balti masala mix (see page 31), or any commercial curry powder, combined with enough water to form a stiff paste. Leave to stand for 10 minutes before using. Add to the recipe where it says masala paste, but allow it to cook for 5 minutes before adding the meat.

CHEF'S TIP 2

Offal can be substituted for meat in any of the meat recipes which follow. It does not require par-cooking, and is added raw. For example, in the previous recipe the offal is added raw and diced at stage 3, in place of the par-cooked meat. The offal is ready at the end of stage 5, so stage 6 is omitted.

BALTI METHI GOSHT

— ♦ —

To the 'standard' Balti meat recipe, we add some pungent spices, especially fenugreek (*methi*, pronounced 'may-tee') leaf and seed. The resultant curry is very savoury and typical of the Balti area.

Serves 4 *(makes 4 portions)*

4 portions par-cooked Balti meat (see page 45)

2–3 tablespoons ghee or corn oil
3–6 garlic cloves, finely chopped
8 oz (225 g) onion, very finely chopped
3–4 tablespoons Balti masala paste (see page 38)
about 7 fl oz (200 ml) reserved stock (see page 45), Balti chicken stock (see page 65) or water
1 tablespoon Balti garam masala (see page 33)

1 tablespoon very finely chopped fresh coriander leaves
aromatic salt to taste (see page 34)

SPICES 1
1 teaspoon fenugreek seeds
1 teaspoon white cummin seeds
$^1/_2$ teaspoon black onion seeds

SPICES 2
1 tablespoon dry fenugreek leaf, ground, or 4 tablespoons fresh fenugreek leaf, de-stalked and chopped

1 Heat the ghee or the oil in your karahi on high heat. Stir-fry **Spices 1** for 20 seconds, then add the garlic and continue stir-frying for a further 30 seconds.

2 Add the onion on a reduced heat. Stir-fry for 10 minutes, allowing the onion to become translucent and begin to brown.

3 Add the masala paste and the par-cooked meat. Raise the heat again and bring to a brisk sizzle, stir-frying as needed for about 5 minutes.

4 Add **Spices 2** and the stock or water, and simmer, stirring, on a lower heat for about 10 minutes.

5 Test for tenderness. If more cooking is needed, add stock or water as required. When as you like it, add the garam masala, fresh coriander leaves and aromatic salt to taste. Simmer for 15 minutes more, then serve.

BALTI SAG GOSHT

— ♦ —

This combination of tastes – meat and spinach (*sag*) with savoury spices – creates another typical authentic dish from the region.

Serves 4 *(makes 4 portions)*

2¹/₂-3 portions par-cooked Balti meat (see page 45)

2–3 tablespoons ghee or corn oil
3–6 garlic cloves, finely chopped
8 oz (225 g) onion, very finely chopped
3–4 tablespoons Balti masala paste (see page 38)
1 lb (450 g) fresh spinach leaves, or 8 oz (225 g) frozen and thawed spinach leaves
about 7 fl oz (200 ml) reserved stock (see page 45), Balti chicken stock (see page 65) or water

1 tablespoon Balti garam masala (see page 33)
1 tablespoon very finely chopped fresh coriander leaves
aromatic salt to taste (see page 34)

SPICES
2 teaspoons white cummin seeds
1 teaspoon black mustard seeds
1 teaspoon yellow mustard powder
¹/₂ teaspoon ground cinnamon

1 Heat the ghee or oil in your karahi on high heat, then stir-fry the **Spices** for 20 seconds. Add the garlic and continue stir-frying for a further 30 seconds.

2 Add the onion on a reduced heat. Stir-fry for 10 minutes, allowing the onion to become translucent and begin to brown.

3 Add the masala paste and the par-cooked meat. Raise the heat again, and bring to a brisk sizzle, stir-frying as needed for about 5 minutes. Add the spinach and the stock or water, and simmer, stirring, on a lower heat for about 10 minutes.

4 Test for tenderness. If more cooking is needed, add stock or water as required. When as you like it, add the garam masala, fresh coriander leaves and aromatic salt to taste. Simmer for 15 minutes more, then serve.

BALTI LAHORI GOSHT

—— ◆ ——

Lahore is in the north of Pakistan, quite near the Indian border. In the days of the great Moghul Emperors, Lahore was a major city connecting Agra and Delhi in the south-west and the Emperors' summer retreat of Kashmir in the north. A great tree-lined road was especially built to facilitate the Emperor's mighty bi-annual procession between these cities, involving hundreds of elephants, thousands of camels and horses, and tens of thousands of camp followers. Every night a new camp was built and the cooking begun.

This creamy aromatic dish would have been one they enjoyed, served with pullao rice and chutneys.

Serves 4 *(makes 4 portions)*

4 portions par-cooked Balti meat (see page 45)

2–3 tablespoons ghee or corn oil
3–6 garlic cloves, finely chopped
8 oz (225 g) onion, very finely chopped
3–4 tablespoons Balti masala paste (see page 38)
about 7 fl oz (200 ml) reserved stock (see page 45), Balti chicken stock (see page 65) or water
8 fl oz (250 ml) thick double cream
2 teaspoons granulated sugar

1 tablespoon Balti garam masala (see page 33)
1 tablespoon very finely chopped fresh coriander leaves
aromatic salt to taste (see page 34)

SPICES
1 teaspoon white cummin seeds
1 teaspoon sesame seeds
$1/4$ teaspoon fennel seeds
$1/4$ teaspoon aniseed
6–8 green cardamom seeds
4–6 cloves
2 in (5 cm) piece cassia bark
$1/4$ teaspoon turmeric

1 Heat the ghee or oil in your karahi on high heat, then stir-fry the garlic and **Spices** for 30 seconds.

2 Add the onion on a reduced heat, and stir-fry for about 10 minutes, allowing the onion to become translucent and begin to brown.

3 Add the masala paste and the par-cooked meat. Raise the heat again and bring to a brisk sizzle, stir-frying as needed for about 5 minutes.

4 Add the reserved stock or water bit by bit and simmer, stirring, on a lower heat for about 10 minutes.

5 Add the cream and sugar, and test for tenderness. If more cooking is needed add stock or water as required. When as you like it, add the garam masala, fresh coriander leaves and aromatic salt to taste.

6 Simmer for 15 minutes more, then serve.

CHEF'S TIP

Remember, Balti is usually eaten as a combination of ingredients. All the meat recipes in this chapter can be treated as 'combination' recipes by simply adding any other cooked 'main' ingredients of your choice – for example, uncooked chicken, seafood and/or vegetables.

Always use a total uncooked weight of 1¹/₂ lb (675 g) of your main ingredients to serve four. So if you add a quantity of chicken, for example, remember to decrease the quantity of meat you use by the same amount. Chapter 7 gives some suggested combinations.

BALTI PESHAWARI GOSHT

— ◆ —

One of the great influences on Balti cooking came from the Frontier area of Pakistan, and the Pathan people. One of the most significant towns in this rugged, tough mountainous area is Peshwar, where rails, roads and travellers converge.

Nuts, raisins and sugar give a hint that this recipe has an Iranian feeling as well as a Pathan influence.

Serves 4 *(makes 4 portions)*

4 portions par-cooked Balti meat (see page 45)

2–3 tablespoons ghee or corn oil
3–6 garlic cloves, finely chopped
2 in (5 cm) cube fresh ginger, chopped
8 oz (225 g) onion, very finely chopped
3–4 tablespoons Balti masala paste (see page 38)
about 7 fl oz (200 ml) reserved stock (see page 45), Balti chicken stock (see page 65) or water

4 oz (110 g) whole almonds, blanched and peeled
4 tablespoons raisins
1 tablespoon dark molasses sugar
1 tablespoon Balti garam masala (see page 33)
1 tablespoon very finely chopped fresh coriander leaves
aromatic salt to taste (see page 34)

SPICES
2–4 brown cardamoms
2 in (5 cm) piece cassia bark
2–3 star anise

1 Heat the ghee or oil in your karahi on high heat, then stir-fry the **Spices** for 20 seconds before adding the garlic and stir-frying for a further 30 seconds. Then add the ginger and continue stir-frying for a further minute.

2 Add the onion on a reduced heat, and stir-fry for about 10 minutes, allowing the onion to become translucent and begin to brown.

3 Add the masala paste and the par-cooked meat. Raise the heat again and bring to a brisk sizzle, stir-frying as needed for about 5 minutes.

4   Add the stock, almonds, raisins and sugar, and simmer, stirring, on a lower heat for about 10 minutes.

5   Test for tenderness. If more cooking is needed, add stock or water as required. When as you like it, add the garam masala, fresh coriander leaves and aromatic salt to taste.

6   Simmer for 15 minutes more, then serve.

BALTI KHYBER GOSHT
— ♦ —

This delightfully tangy meat dish is made unique by the combination of yoghurt and spices.

Serves 4 *(makes 4 portions)*

4 portions par-cooked Balti meat (see page 45)

2–3 tablespoons ghee or corn oil
3–6 garlic cloves, finely chopped
8 oz (225 g) onion, very finely chopped
3–4 tablespoons Balti masala paste (see page 38)
about 7 fl oz (200 ml) reserved stock (see page 45), Balti chicken stock (see page 65) or water
7 oz (200 ml) Greek yoghurt

1 tablespoon Balti garam masala (see page 33)
1 tablespoon very finely chopped fresh coriander leaves
aromatic salt to taste (see page 34)

SPICES (roasted, then ground)
1 teaspoon white cummin seeds
1 teaspoon green cardamom seeds
6 cloves
2 in (5 cm) piece cassia bark

1   Heat the ghee or oil in your karahi on high heat, then stir-fry the **Spices** for 20 seconds, before adding the garlic and stir-frying for a further 30 seconds.

2   Add the onion on a reduced heat, and stir-fry for about 10 minutes, allowing the onion to become translucent and begin to brown.

3 Add the masala paste and the par-cooked meat. Raise the heat again and bring to a brisk sizzle, stir-frying as needed for about 5 minutes.

4 Add the stock or water, and simmer, stirring, on a lower heat for about 10 minutes.

5 Add the yoghurt and test for tenderness. If more cooking is needed add stock or water as required. When as you like it, add the garam masala, fresh coriander leaves and aromatic salt to taste. Simmer for 15 minutes more, then serve.

BALTI PERSIAN GOSHT
— ♦ —

There is much Persian influence in the cooking of the Balti region, in particular the addition of dried fruit and sweeteners to meat and savoury dishes. Try eating this with a huge Balti naan bread.

Serves 4 *(makes 4 portions)*

4 portions par-cooked Balti
  meat (see page 45)

2–3 tablespoons ghee or corn oil
3–6 garlic cloves, finely
  chopped
8 oz (225 g) onion, very finely
  chopped
3–4 tablespoons Balti masala
  paste (see page 38)
4 oz (110 g) dried figs
4 oz (110 g) dates, stoned
2 tablespoons pine kernels
2 tablespoons shelled hazelnuts
1 tablespoon clear honey
about 7 fl oz (200 ml) reserved
  stock (see page 45), Balti
  chicken stock (see page 65) or
  water

1 tablespoon Balti garam
  masala (see page 33)
1 tablespoon very finely
  chopped fresh coriander
  leaves
aromatic salt to taste (see page
  34)

SPICES
1 teaspoon cummin seeds,
  roasted
1 teaspoon coriander seeds,
  roasted
1 teaspoon paprika
$1/_2$ teaspoon turmeric
$1/_2$ teaspoon mango powder

1 Heat the ghee or oil in your karahi on high heat, and stir-fry the **Spices** for 20 seconds, then add the garlic and continue to stir-fry for a further 30 seconds.

2 Add the onion on a reduced heat, and stir-fry for about 10 minutes, allowing the onion to become translucent and begin to brown.

3 Add the masala paste and the par-cooked meat. Raise the heat again and bring to a brisk sizzle, stir-frying as needed for about 5 minutes.

4 Add the dried fruit, pine kernels, nuts and honey, along with the stock or water, and simmer, stirring, on a lower heat for about 10 minutes.

5 Test for tenderness. If more cooking is needed add stock or water as required. When as you like it, add the garam masala, fresh coriander leaves and aromatic salt to taste.

6 Simmer for 15 minutes more, then serve.

BALTI MINCE (KEEMA)

— ♦ —

Simple minced beef (or indeed any minced meat – for example lamb, pork, or venison) makes the most delicious Balti dish. Mince is almost indestructible in the cooking process, so it simply cannot be overcooked. It is therefore a great dish for the beginner.

Serve 4 *(makes 4 portions)*

1½ lb (675 g) minced meat

2 tablespoons ghee or corn oil
4 garlic cloves, finely chopped
8 oz (225 g) onion, finely chopped
3 tablespoons Balti masala paste (see page 38)

1 tablespoon tomato purée
1 tablespoon Balti garam masala (see page 33)
1 tablespoon chopped fresh coriander leaves
aromatic salt to taste (see page 34)

1 Put the mince into the karahi and stir-fry it for 10 minutes. This 'seals' it and draws off liquids. Strain off and reserve the liquid.

2 Heat the ghee or oil in your karahi on high heat. Stir-fry the garlic for 30 seconds.

3 Add the onion, reduce the heat and stir-fry for about 10 minutes, allowing it to become translucent and begin to brown.

4 Add the masala paste and the tomato purée. Raise the heat and bring to a brisk sizzle, stir-frying for about 2–3 minutes.

5 Add the mince to the karahi and stir-fry it until it is sizzling.

6 Simmer uncovered for 35–40 minutes. Little by little add the reserved liquid (and, if needed, some water) to ensure it is not sticking, and to achieve a nice creamy texture.

7 Add the garam masala, coriander leaves and aromatic salt to taste. It is ready to serve after a few minutes, but can be kept simmering until needed.

Opposite: Balti Zeera Harsha (page 70)

BALTI KEEMA TANDOORI

— ◆ —

This variation on the previous recipe is really delicious, combining Balti and Tandoori tastes in one dish.

Serves 4 (makes 4 portions)

1¹/₂ (675g) minced meat

2 tablespoons ghee or corn oil
4 garlic cloves, finely chopped
8 oz (225 g) onion, finely chopped
3 tablespoons tandoori masala paste (see page 39)
1 tablespoon tomato pureé
3 oz (75g) Greek yoghurt

1 tablespoon Balti garam masala (see page 33)
1 tablespoon fresh coriander leaves, chopped
aromatic salt to taste (see page 34)

SPICES
1 teaspoon cummin seeds
¹/₂ teaspoon aniseed

1 Put the mince into the karahi and stir-fry it for 10 minutes. This 'seals' it and draws off liquids. Strain off and reserve the liquid.

2 Heat the ghee or oil in your karahi on high heat. Stir-fry the **Spices** for 10 seconds then add the garlic and stir-fry for 30 seconds.

3 Add the onion, reduce the heat and stir-fry for about 10 minutes, allowing it to become translucent and begin to brown.

4 Add the tandoori masala paste and the tomato pureé. Raise the heat and bring to a brisk sizzle, stir-frying as needed for about 2–3 minutes.

5 Add the mince to the karahi and stir-fry it until it is sizzling.

6 Simmer uncovered for 35–40 minutes. Little by little add the reserved liquid and yoghurt to ensure it is not sticking, and to achieve a nice creamy texture.

7 Add the garam masala, coriander and aromatic salt to taste. It is ready to serve after a few minutes, but can be kept simmering until needed.

Opposite: Balti Grilled Fish (page 84), served with Balti Salad (page 146)

CHAPTER · 3

Poultry and Game

In the rugged Balti lands chicken is a much loved dish. It is eaten quite regularly, as are game birds when caught. Game birds offer an excellent change from domestic poultry, and all are ideal for Balti cooking.

In the recipes in this chapter I have specified a particular type of meat, whether duck, chicken or game bird, but these are just suggestions to start you off. You could use any of the birds mentioned in this introduction.

DOMESTIC POULTRY

The domestic chicken is said to have originated in India. Early on in man's route to civilisation it attached itself to the camp-site for easy feeding, and soon become domesticated, at least as early as 8,000 BC in Mesopotamia. We know that the civilisation which inhabited the Indus Valley bred chickens in 4,500 BC, and that the Ancient Egyptians operated egg hatcheries and incubators 2,000 years later. The world of the battery hen is very ancient, and the duck, goose and turkey have also been domesticated for thousands of years.

The argument about battery hens and free-range is loud and emotive. 'Corn-fed' chicken can be an acronym for free-range, but it does not follow that the hens are running about the farmyard scratching at grains of corn scattered by the farmer's wife. They are just as likely to be battery corn-fed. The yellow colour of the flesh can also be induced by feeding turmeric or tartrazine.

Chicken

The most popular of all meat and especially good in Balti dishes, chicken is classified according to its age and weight at slaughter.

We start eating chicken at 4–6 weeks when it is called *Poussin* and weighs 1–1¼ lb (450–550 g). These tiny birds are best cooked on the bone and will yield just enough meat for one.

Double Poussin is aged between 6 and 10 weeks and at 1½–2 lb (675–900 g) serves two, cooked on the bone.

Spring or Broiling (Grilling) Chicken is aged around 3–4 months and weighs 2½–3½ lb (1.1–1.5 kg). It yields three or four servings.

Roasting Chicken is aged up to a year and weighs 3½–4½ lb (1.5–2 kg). It will serve four to six people.

Boiling Chicken is over a year old and weighs 4–8 lb (1.8–3.6 kg). It will serve five to seven people.

Capon is a neutered cockerel over 6 months old, weighing 4–10 lb (1.8–4.5 kg), and will serve five to ten people.

Poularde is a neutered hen over 6 months, with virtually the same characteristics as the capon. Both the above are generally bred to produce very tender white flesh.

Filleted breast meat often comes from a capon or poularde, and will weigh about 6–10 oz (175–300 g), trimmed and fat-free. It is very lean, and is high in iron and protein.

Chicken used in Balti recipes must be skinless.

Duck

It was the Chinese who domesticated the duck in the years before Christ. The most common domestic duck is the white Aylesbury with the yellow beak. Duckling are young duck up to 6 months old, and the carcass is about 3–4 lb (1.3–1.8 kg) in weight. Above that age, duck carcasses weigh in from 4 lb (1.8 kg) to as much as 6 lb (2.7 kg).

The meat yield from duckling and duck is quite small, a high proportion of the weight being in the skin and the rather excessive fat domestic breeding creates. It is essential for Balti cooking to remove all fat and skin.

Magret de Canard This is a French term meaning the lean portion (of a fat duck), and refers to duck breasts, filleted, with skin and fat still attached (which you or your poulterer must pare away). The resultant meat, though expensive, is the best for Balti cooking.

Goose

The grey domestic goose is probably descended from the wild greylag and the white from the snow goose. The goose was farmed by the Ancient Egyptians and Romans.

Goose yields less meat per equal weight of carcass than turkey, but it has a 'gamier' flavour. A goose is table-ready at just 3 months, when it will weigh about 6 lb (2.7 kg). A slightly older bird at 8 lb (3.6 kg) will yield enough meat for four to five people. Goose can be obtained at weights up to 26 lb (11.75 kg) for the special occasion, but it can be tough.

Turkey

It was not until the Spaniards conquered the Americas in the 16th century that the turkey was 'discovered'. They called this enormous bird the 'Indian chicken', because they presumed they were in India. The Aztecs had domesticated it long before the arrival of the Spaniards.

The best turkey in the UK is the Norfolk Black. A plump dressed hen weighs as little as 6 lb (2.7 kg), and serves four to five people. Older birds can weigh up to 30 lb (13.5 kg).

Turkey is excellent for Balti cooking. Use leg meat or breast on or off the bone, but always skinned and without fat.

GAME BIRDS

There is a wide choice of game birds, and many – grouse, guinea fowl, partridge, pheasant, pigeon and quail – are widely available. Most are seasonal, except for pigeon and quail.

In France and the sub-continent wild birds as small as warblers, larks and moorhen are eaten. The peacock (a Middle-Eastern descendant of the pheasant) was prized in Britain at the time of the Crusaders. It is protected in the Indian sub-continent now, and may not be eaten, although I have in my collection peacock recipes from the Maharajas. Swan was equally highly regarded in the Middle Ages, and was to be found on British royal tables until relatively recently.

As Balti cooking derived from the nomadic and unpredictable life of the hunter warrior, game birds are perfect Balti subjects.

Grouse

Of several species of grouse, all ground-living, it is the Scottish or red grouse which is the most sought after for flavour. The average carcass weighs $1\frac{1}{2}$ lb (675 g) and yields a generous single portion of meat.

Guinea Fowl

This is the bird from which all our domestic chicken are presumed to have descended. It is related to the pheasant, and similar in taste, but is slightly larger. A carcass weighs from $2\frac{1}{4}$–$3\frac{1}{2}$ lb (1–1.5 kg).

Partridge

Another relative of the pheasant, the grey-legged partridge is the most common game bird. The carcass weighs from 12–14 oz (350–400 g) and will serve one.

Pheasant

The most popular game bird, the young female provides the tenderest meat with the best flavour. Its carcass averages $2\frac{1}{2}$ lb (1.1 kg) in weight, and should serve three. The cock bird is slightly larger at 3 lb (1.3 kg), but its meat is generally tougher, drier and yields less.

Pigeon

The rock dove is the ancestor of the domestic pigeon. It has pale flesh which is not unlike chicken. Wild (wood) pigeon is larger, with darker, stronger-flavoured meat. Squab is young pigeon, bred for the table. At just 1 month it weighs 12 oz (350 g). An adult weighs from 1–$1\frac{1}{2}$ lb (450–675 g). One small bird will serve one person, a larger one, two people.

Quail

These tiny birds originated in the Middle East but are now found world-wide. Many are farm reared. At just 4–5 oz (100–150 g) per carcass, they should be cooked whole, with the skin on, and will yield enough meat at one per person for a starter, or two for a main course. They are available boned (a fiddly and difficult task to do oneself) and, as such, are delightful stuffed.

Snipe

Another very tiny bird, of approximately the same weight as the quail. They are less commonly available, but a good game dealer should be able to acquire them during the season. Like quail, they are cooked whole, with skin on.

Wild Duck

Mallard, pintail, teal and widgeon are the commonest type of wild duck shot in Britain. There is quite a weight variation between species, and the largest, the mallard, is considerably smaller than a domestic duck. A mallard at $2^1/_2$ lb (1.1 kg) will just serve three. A teal at 12 oz (350 g) is enough for a single portion.

Woodcock

This is a water bird, similar to the snipe. It is quite scarce. At 5 oz (150 g) per carcass, it yields sufficient meat for a starter for one.

BALTI POULTRY COOKING METHODS

Traditional cooking of poultry would be whole and on the bone. Early Baltistan had no ovens, and cooking would be done slowly over embers. Like the Balti restaurants, I have adapted whole birds to Western methods using the traditional marinades, where appropriate, and the oven and aluminium foil. Boneless, diced poultry cooks very fast by the stir-fry method in the Balti cooking pan, and so there are recipes for boneless meat too. Most recipes specify chicken, but usually any poultry or game meat can be substituted (see footnotes to recipes).

Joints can also be used in some recipes, and I have indicated which these are in footnotes to the relevant recipes. You will need to adjust the cooking times accordingly (see below).

Whether whole, joints or fillets, poultry should always be skinned for use in Balti cooking. The only exceptions are quail and snipe.

Cooking Whole Birds

Whole birds require oven baking, the timing of which relates to carcass weight. Here are baking times for whole carcasses, in an oven preheated to 375°F/190°C/Gas 5.

4–5 oz (110–150 g) – 15 minutes (i.e quail, snipe and woodcock)

12–14 oz (350–400 g) – 20–30 minutes (i.e. partridge, squab)

1 lb (450 g) – 40 minutes

Weights over 1 lb (450 g) – Initial 40 minutes for the first 1 lb (450 g) plus 4 minutes per extra $\frac{1}{4}$ lb (4 oz or 100 g). For example a 4 lb (1.8 kg) bird will require 40 + 12 x 4 minutes = just 2 minutes short of $1\frac{1}{2}$ hours.

Cooking Poultry Joints

Poultry joints can also be used in Balti dishes. Timings will vary depending on the size of the joint: 4–5 oz (110–150 g) joints require 15 minutes simmering after the initial stir-fry; 8 oz (225 g) joints require 20–25 minutes simmering; and 12–14 oz (350–400 g) joints require 25–30 minutes simmering. Remember always to skin the joint first and remove as much fat as you can. It is unnecessary to chop joints into small pieces, particularly as the bone will probably splinter. It is important to cook the joint right through so that there is no pink or rare meat. When poultry is cooked correctly, the flesh will come off the bone easily.

Four pairs of joints are cut from a single bird:

Thigh
The leg between the carcass and above the knee joint. Whitish meat and quite juicy.

Drumstick
The lower leg of the fowl, below the knee and above the ankle, in the shape of a pestle. The meat is darker than and inferior to thigh meat.

Back
This is halved so that each half contains an identical piece of white breast.

Wing
This should be cut away from the back at an angle so that it contains some white breast meat.

Note: An alternative cut provides only five joints. The thigh and drumstick are kept together and the back is not halved.

Cooking Diced Poultry

Chicken meat is most popular filleted, skinned and diced into 'bite-sized' cubes, and the most popular (and therefore the most expensive) cut is breast. It is white when cooked, extremely tender and has good flavour, particularly if you can obtain a genuine free-range bird. Thigh meat is darker than breast, and drumstick meat is reddest of all. Even so, it is less fat saturated than red meat, so is perceived to be 'healthier'.

The meat of other large birds such as turkey, goose and duck, can also be diced. Turkey is slightly tougher than chicken, but is markedly cheaper. Goose and duck are more fatty than chicken or turkey, so need to be very well trimmed.

The best dice size for Balti poultry meat (filleted and skinless) is about $1^{1}/_{4}$ in (3 cm) cubes. Obviously it is not possible to cut exactly square dice of even size, but make that the average size.

Although jointed and filleted poultry meat is now readily available (and will be prepared to your requirements by a reputable poulterer), it will be much cheaper if you buy a dressed carcass and joint or fillet it to your own requirements. It is neither unpleasant nor difficult to do this.

Poultry Giblets

Even the largest bird yields only a small amount of offal compared with meat. The modern poulterer supplies the liver, kidneys and heart along with the neck in a plastic bag stored inside the bird's cavity. Do remember to remove this, although it won't be the first time that these stay inside the bird while it oven roasts! (Melted plastic does nothing to enhance the flavour of the meat!)

Use the neck for stock (see opposite). The liver, kidneys and heart are best kept frozen until you have a number of them. They will then make a great Balti stir-fry dish (if you substitute them for the meat in the recipes on pages 66, 68, 69, 70).

BALTI CHICKEN STOCK

— ♦ —

After filleting a dressed bird there is still plenty of goodness left. Make it into Balti stock. This recipe uses a dressed roasting chicken weighing around 4 lb (1.8 kg), but you could use pheasant, turkey or any other bird. Add the neck if you have it.

Makes about 1¹/₂ pints (900 ml)

1 oven-ready chicken, about
   4 lb (1.8 kg) in weight

6 garlic cloves, quartered
4 oz (110 g) onion, coarsely
   sliced
4 bay leaves
1 tablespoon Balti masala paste
   (see page 38)

2 celery sticks, chopped
1 large carrot, chopped
1 tablespoon sugar
1 teaspoon salt
2 pints (1.1 litre) water

1 Remove and discard the skin from the carcass. It will pull off relatively easily. Use a knife or kitchen scissors as needed.

2 Cut off the best of the meat, in pieces as large as you can get. Keep covered in the refrigerator, or freeze for use in another recipe.

3 Cut the carcass into joints that will fit comfortably into a large lidded pot.

4 Put in all the remaining ingredients and bring to the boil.

5 Lower the heat, put the lid on, and maintain a rolling simmer for 30 minutes or so. Check, and add more water if needed. Continue simmering for 30 more minutes.

6 Strain the stock, and discard the solids. Leave to cool.

7 Pour about 7 fl oz (200 ml) into a yoghurt pot or equivalent. Repeat, using further pots, until all the stock is poured out, then freeze for 24 hours.

8 Break the stock out of the moulds, put in a lidded container and straight back into the freezer. Use as required.

BALTI CHICKEN, MEDIUM HEAT

— ♦ —

This is a 'standard', medium-heat Balti preparation. It will result in tender, bite-sized cubes of chicken in ample golden brown spicy gravy, neither too hot, nor too mild.

Serves 4 *(makes 4 portions)*

1¹/₂ lb (675 g) skinned and boned chicken meat (weighed after discarding unwanted matter), diced into 1¹/₄ in (3 cm) cubes

2–3 tablespoons ghee or corn oil
3–6 garlic cloves, finely chopped
8 oz (225 g) onion, very finely chopped

3–4 tablespoons Balti masala paste (see page 38)
1 cupful (about 7 fl oz/200 ml) Balti chicken stock (see page 65) or water
1 tablespoon Balti garam masala (see page 33)
1 tablespoon very finely chopped fresh coriander leaves
aromatic salt to taste (see page 34)

1 Heat the ghee or oil in your karahi on high heat, then stir-fry the garlic for 30 seconds.

2 Add the onion, reduce the heat, and stir-fry for about 10 minutes, allowing the onion to become translucent and begin to brown.

3 Add the masala paste and the chicken. Raise the heat again and bring to a brisk sizzle, stir-frying as needed for about 5 minutes.

4 Add about a cupful of stock or water, and simmer, stirring, on a lower heat for about 10 minutes.

5 Test that the chicken is cooked right through by removing a piece and cutting it in two. If there are any traces of pink, replace the halves in the pan and continue cooking. Keep testing. When cooked as you like it, add the garam masala, fresh coriander leaves and salt to taste.

Note: This recipe can be used for any boneless poultry or game. Adjust times accordingly: duck, for instance, will take about 10 minutes longer to cook than chicken or turkey.

BALTI CHICKEN TIKKA MASALA

— ♦ —

This is the Balti house version of the UK's most popular curry dish.

***Serves 4** (makes 4 portions)*

1¹/₂ lb (675 g) skinned and boned
    chicken meat (weighed after
    discarding unwanted matter),
    cut into 1¹/₄ in (3 cm) cubes
3 tablespoons ghee or corn oil
3–6 garlic cloves, finely
    chopped
8 oz (225 g) onion, very finely
    chopped
3–4 tablespoons Balti masala
    paste (see page 38)
about 7 fl oz (200 ml) Balti
    chicken stock (see page 65)
    or water
1 tablespoon Balti garam
    masala (see page 33)

1 tablespoon very finely
    chopped fresh coriander
    leaves
aromatic salt to taste (see page
    34)

MARINADE
10 oz (300 g) Greek yoghurt
1 tablespoon dry fenugreek
    leaves, ground
1 tablespoon dried mint,
    ground
2 tablespoons tandoori masala
    paste (see page 39)
¹/₂ teaspoon orange or red food
    colouring (optional)
¹/₂ teaspoon salt

1 Mix together the marinade ingredients in a non-metallic bowl.
   Immerse the chicken pieces, cover and refrigerate for 24 hours.

2 After the marination, heat a tablespoon of ghee in the karahi.
   Spoon half the chicken and its marinade into the karahi and
   briskly stir-fry for 5 minutes. Remove and repeat with the other
   half, using another tablespoon of ghee.

3 Wipe the karahi clean and heat the final tablespoon of ghee.
   Stir-fry the garlic for 30 seconds.

4 Add the onion, reduce the heat and stir-fry for about 10 minutes,
   allowing the onion to become translucent and begin to brown.

5 Add the masala paste, and the chicken, along with the stock.
   Simmer, stirring, on a lowish heat for about 10 minutes. When
   cooked right through, add the garam masala, fresh coriander
   leaves and aromatic salt to taste.

Note: You may use any poultry or game meat or joints for this
recipe (see pages 58–64).

JASHASHA HUNZA BALTIT

— ♦ —

A 600-year-old fort now guards the hill town of Hunza Baltit, but other forts had existed for centuries beforehand. Built in the Tibetan style, this aged building is a reminder that the Silk Route once ran through here, linking China to the Mediterranean. This dish has Chino-Tibetan roots – the basis of true Balti cooking.

Serves 4 *(makes 4 portions)*

1½ lb (675 g) chicken meat, weighed after boning and skinning, cut into 1¼ in (3 cm) cubes

2–3 tablespoons ghee or corn oil
3–6 garlic cloves, finely chopped
8 oz (225 g) onion, very finely chopped
3–4 tablespoons Balti masala paste (see page 38)
about 7 fl oz (200 ml) Balti chicken stock (see page 65) or water
8 oz (225 g) cooked beetroot (not bottled), peeled and cut into shreds

1 tablespoon dark molasses sugar
1 teaspoon soy sauce
1 tablespoon Balti garam masala (see page 33)
1 tablespoon very finely chopped fresh coriander leaves
aromatic salt to taste (see page 34)

SPICES
1 teaspoon fennel seeds
2–3 star anise
2 in (5 cm) piece cassia bark
4–6 cloves

1 Heat the ghee or oil in your karahi on high heat, then stir-fry the garlic and the **Spices** for 30 seconds.

2 Add the onion, reduce the heat and stir-fry for 10 minutes, allowing the onion to become translucent and begin to brown.

3 Add the masala paste and the chicken. Raise the heat again and bring to a brisk sizzle, stir-frying as needed for about 5 minutes.

4 Add the stock or water bit by bit, along with the beetroot, and soy sauce. Simmer, stirring, on a lower heat for about 10 minutes.

5 Test that the chicken is cooked right through by cutting into one of the pieces (see stage 5 on page 66). When cooked as you like it, add the garam masala, coriander and aromatic salt.

Note: You may substitute any poultry or game meat or joints for this recipe (see pages 58–64).

BALTI MURGH SKARDU
— ♦ —

The capital of Baltistan is the town of Skardu. It has a population of a few thousand, plenty of hybrid milking cows (*dzos*), a polo ground, a fortress, the River Indus and, once, a royal family. It has a few cheap hotels and restaurants. This chicken dish with its aromatic spices and cream is typical of the tastes of Baltistan.

Serves 4 *(makes 4 portions)*

1¹/₂ lb (675 g) skinned and boned chicken meat (weighed after discarding unwanted matter), cut into 1¹/₄ in (3 cm) cubes

2–3 tablespoons ghee or corn oil
3–6 garlic cloves, finely chopped
8 oz (225 g) onion, very finely chopped
3–4 tablespoons Balti masala paste (see page 38)
6 fl oz (175 ml) double cream
2 teaspoons granulated sugar
about 7 fl oz (200 ml) Balti chicken stock (see page 65) or water

1 tablespoon Balti garam masala (see page 33)
1 tablespoon very finely chopped fresh coriander leaves
aromatic salt to taste (see page 34)

SPICES
1 teaspoon sesame seeds
1 teaspoon white poppy seeds
¹/₂ teaspoon fennel seeds
¹/₂ teaspoon lovage seeds
2–3 brown or black cardamom seeds
2 in (5 cm) piece cassia bark

1 Heat the ghee or oil in your karahi on high heat, then stir-fry the garlic and **Spices** for 30 seconds.

2 Add the onion and, reducing the heat, stir-fry for about 10 minutes, allowing the onion to become translucent and begin to brown.

3 Add the masala paste and the chicken. Raise the heat again and bring to a brisk sizzle, stir-frying as needed for about 5 minutes.

4 Add the cream and sugar, along with the stock or water, bit by bit. Simmer, stirring, on a lower heat for about 10 minutes.

5 Test that the chicken is cooked right through by cutting into one of the pieces (see stage 5 on page 66). When cooked as you like it, add the garam masala, fresh coriander and aromatic salt to taste.

Note: You may substitute any poultry or game meat or joints for this recipe (see pages 58–64).

BALTI ZEERA HARSHA
— ♦ —

This tasty stir-fry is of duck breast chunks enhanced by black and white cummin seeds (*zeera*). Its sweet taste is said to have been introduced by Chinese travellers to the Balti district. Duck and other flighted game have always been plentiful and popular in the area.

Serves 4 *(makes 4 portions)*

1¹/₂ lb (675 g) skinned and boned duck breast meat (weighed after discarding unwanted matter and removing excess fat), cut into 1¹/₄ in (3 cm) cubes	*1 tablespoon chopped fresh mint*
	about 7 fl oz (200 ml) Balti chicken stock (see page 65), or water

1¹/₂ lb (675 g) skinned and boned duck breast meat (weighed after discarding unwanted matter and removing excess fat), cut into 1¹/₄ in (3 cm) cubes

2–3 tablespoons ghee or corn oil
3–6 garlic cloves, finely chopped
8 oz (225 g) onion, very finely chopped
3–4 tablespoons Balti masala paste (see page 38)
14 oz (400 g) tinned plum tomatoes, strained
12 fresh tangerine segments, chopped

1 tablespoon chopped fresh mint
about 7 fl oz (200 ml) Balti chicken stock (see page 65), or water
1 tablespoon Balti garam masala (see page 33)
1 tablespoon very finely chopped fresh coriander leaves
aromatic salt to taste (see page 34)

SPICES
1 teaspoon white cummin seeds
¹/₂ teaspoon black cummin seeds
¹/₂ teaspoon wild onion seeds

1 Heat the ghee or oil in your karahi on high heat, then stir-fry the garlic and **Spices** for 30 seconds.

2 Add the onion and, reducing the heat, stir-fry for about 10 minutes, allowing the onion to become translucent and begin to brown.

3 Add the masala paste and the duck. Raise the heat again and bring to a brisk sizzle, stir-frying as needed for about 5 minutes.

4 Add the tomatoes, tangerine segments and mint. Add the stock or water, bit by bit, and simmer, stirring, on a lower heat for about 20 minutes.

5 Test that the duck is cooked right through by cutting into one of the pieces (see stage 5 on page 66). When cooked as you like it, add the garam masala, fresh coriander and aromatic salt to taste.

Note: You can substitute any poultry or game meat or joints for this recipe (see pages 58–64).

BALTI TURKEY CURRY

— ♦ —

Thanks to efficient farming turkey is readily available all year round and it is cheap. Skinned breast, thigh or leg can be used in this recipe, off-the-bone.

Serves 4 (makes 4 portions)

1½ lb (675 g) skinned and boned turkey meat (weighed after discarding unwanted matter), diced into 1¼ in (3 cm) cubes.

3 tablespoons ghee or corn oil
4–6 garlic cloves, finely chopped
8 oz (225 g) onion, very finely chopped
2 tablespoons Balti masala paste (see page 38)
1 tablespoon green masala paste (see page 39)

1 tablespoon tandoori masala paste (see page 39)
6–8 tomatoes, chopped
1 cupful (about 7 fl oz/200 ml) Balti chicken stock (see page 65), or water
1 cupful Balti garam masala (see page 33)
1 tablespoon fresh coriander leaves, very finely chopped
aromatic salt to taste (see page 34)

1 Heat the ghee or oil in your karahi on high heat. Stir-fry the garlic for 30 seconds.

2 Add the onion, reduce the heat and stir-fry for about 10 minutes, allowing it to become translucent and begin to brown.

3 Add the pastes and the turkey. Raise the heat and bring to a brisk sizzle, stir-frying as needed for about 5 minutes.

4 Add about a cupful of stock or water. Simmer, reduce the heat and stir-fry for about 20 minutes.

5 Test that the turkey is cooked right through by cutting into one of the pieces (see stage 5 on page 66). If more cooking is needed, keep testing. When it is as you like it, add the garam masala, fresh coriander leaves and aromatic salt to taste.

BALTI MURGH MASALA

— ♦ —

This dish requires a whole chicken to be baked (or roasted). First it is skinned then marinated.

Traditionally Baltistan had no ovens, but the ancient tribesmen did not lack ideas. The fire on the ground would be raked out. The marinated chicken would be covered in leaves, then with muddy clay. It would be placed directly into the embers and covered with them, and it would slow cook for several hours. The clay would then be cracked off, and the baked bird eaten, leaves and all. Delicious!

Here's a modern interpretation requiring much less effort than it looks.

Following this recipe is a variation using quail or snipe instead of chicken. The recipe is the same, but the cooking time is much shorter.

Serves 4 *(makes 4 portions)*

1 x 4 lb (1.8 kg) roasting
    chicken, skinned (optionally
    boned), giblets removed
20–25 large spinach leaves,
    stalks trimmed

MARINADE
3 tablespoons Balti masala
    paste (see page 38)
1 tablespoon Balti garam
    masala (see page 33)
0–2 teaspoons chilli powder
    (optional)

1 tablespoon finely chopped
    fresh mint leaves
1 tablespoon finely chopped
    fresh coriander leaves
3 garlic cloves, finely chopped
10 oz (300 g) Greek yoghurt
1 teaspoon salt

STUFFING
6–8 oz (175–225 g) cooked plain
    rice

1 Wash the chicken clean inside and out, then pat dry with kitchen paper. Make small incisions with your knife point into the deepest parts of the flesh.

2 Mix the marinade ingredients together.

3 Coat the chicken generously with the marinade. Place it in a non-metallic lidded container, put the lid on and refrigerate for 24 hours.

4 After that time, soften the spinach by steaming it for a minute, or microwaving for 30 seconds. Preheat the oven to 375°F/190°C/Gas 5.

5 Stuff the centre of the chicken with the cold rice, then re-coat it with any excess marinade.

6 Carefully and thoroughly cover the chicken with the softened spinach leaves. Keep on adding leaves until they are used up.

7 Gingerly wrap the whole thing with kitchen foil. Put the chicken on a rack above an oven tray in the oven.

8 Bake for about $1^1/_2$ hours (see page 63). Check that it is cooked by removing the foil over a leg area and moving the leaves. Poke a small knife blade into the flesh and if the liquid runs out clear, the chicken is ready. If the juices are pink, replace the leaves and foil and continue cooking in the oven for a few minutes more.

BALTI QUAIL OR SNIPE
— ◆ —

These tiny delicious game birds are superb roasted. For this recipe the quails can be on or off the bone – ask your butcher to bone them for you as it's a fiddly job. Snipe can be used alternatively. Allow two per person.

Serves 4 (makes 4 portions)

Follow the previous recipe using 8 quail or snipe in place of the chicken. Do not remove the skin.

At stage 6, cover each individual quail or snipe with the spinach leaves then place on an oven tray and cover the tray with kitchen foil. Bake for 15 minutes.

BALTI PHEASANT

— ◆ —

This delicious authentic north Pakistani dish is a variation of the whole baked chicken recipe on page 73. Indeed it would far more likely be pheasant than chicken that was used in Baltistan. Use a female pheasant for a tasty succulent gamey meal. This recipe is for two servings. If you want to serve four, it is better to buy two pheasants of the size given, than to try to find a larger bird which could be tough.

Serves 2 *(makes 2 portions)*

2¼-2½ lb (1–1.1 kg) pheasant 'dressed' and oven ready with skin and giblets removed

15–20 large spinach leaves, stalks trimmed

MARINADE
1 tablespoon Balti masala paste (see page 38)
1 tablespoon tandoori masala paste (see page 39)
0–2 teaspoons chilli powder (optional)

1 tablespoon finely chopped fresh mint
1 tablespoon finely chopped fresh coriander
2 garlic cloves, finely chopped
7 oz (200 g) Greek yoghurt
½ teaspoon salt

STUFFING
6–8 oz (175–225 g) cooked plain rice

Follow the method on page 73 but reduce the baking time in stage 8 to just under an hour for a 2¼ lb (1 kg) bird, and 1 hr 5 minutes for a 2½ lb (1.1 kg) bird.

CHAPTER · 4

Fish and Shellfish

Baltistan is over 900 miles (some 1,400 km) from the sea and, at an average height of 16,000 feet (5,000 metres) above sea level, it seems unlikely that there would be any fish at all in the area. However, it is fed by countless streams pouring down the mountains, and its great river, the Indus, is augmented by other large tributaries. In addition, there are numerous glacial lakes, some quite large.

Thus there is no shortage of freshwater fish and shellfish, and the fishing is excellent. However, there are not many authentic recipes from the area, as the Baltis are not particularly fond of fish.

Reflecting similar reluctance to eat fish in the UK, the Balti house offers fish and shellfish on a limited scale, prawns being a popular option. With the massive amount of fresh and frozen ingredients now available from the fishmongers, and with the home cook's rapidly expanding awareness of the benefits of fish, I feel at liberty to expand the repertoire of Balti-style recipes to include as wide a variety of ingredients as possible.

Not only does fish translate superbly to Balti cooking methods, it is tasty, nutritious and amazingly healthy. It is high in protein, low in cholesterol and a particularly good source of vitamins A, D and E. The oil in fish is polyunsaturated and is regarded as healthier than that in meat.

FISH

Fish is classified into two main types, freshwater fish and sea fish, but there are further categories, such as white fish, oily fish and shellfish.

White Fish

There are two groups of white fish, round and flat. The larger round species are available as steaks, on or off-the-bone – cod, coley, haddock, hake, pollack, etc. Smaller round species such as whiting are sold whole, trimmed, filleted and skinned as required. Other round fish include bass, bream, gurnard, John Dory, ling, monkfish, and grey and red mullet.

The larger flat species such as halibut and turbot are available as filleted steaks. Smaller flat species, which include plaice, lemon and Dover sole, are sold whole, trimmed or filleted as required. Other popular white flat fish include brill, dab, flounder, megrim, skate and witch sole.

Oily Fish

These include many members of the herring family – herring itself, pilchard, sardine (young pilchard), and sprats. Mackerel, smelt and whitebait are also oily fish. Most are sold whole, or in fillets according to size.

Freshwater Fish

The commoner varieties of fish that live in fresh water include carp, grayling, perch, pike, salmon, salmon trout (sea trout), brown trout, and rainbow trout. These are available whole, in steaks or fillets, depending on size. Some have 'white' flesh; some are oily.

Exotic Fish

There are thousands of species of all shapes and sizes. Some of those readily available include barracuda, croaker, drum, emperor bream, grouper, hilsa, pomfret, rayfish, shark, snapper, swordfish, and tuna. They are all warm-water fish, but many are now available fresh, and all are available frozen.

Smoked Fish

Smoking is an ancient preservative method for meat or fish. The item is first coated in salt to leach out moisture, and is then hung to dry. Finally it is placed above a smoking fire. This seals the item and imparts flavour. Any white fish can be smoked and filleted, and smoked haddock translates well to Balti (see page 83).

SHELLFISH

Shelfish is categorised into three groups: molluscs, which are invertebrates protected by a strong shell; crustaceans, which have a skeleton and a shell which varies in toughness from species to species; and cephalopods, which are invertebrates with no shell.

Molluscs

Some molluscs have a single shell, others a hinged double shell (bivalves). The former include limpets, whelks and winkles. The latter includes abalone, clams, mussels, oysters and scallops. The recipe on page 87 uses scallops, and that on page 88 oysters, but you could use any molluscs in their place.

Crustaceans

Crabs, lobsters, crayfish, crawfish, scampi, shrimps and prawns are all part of this group. Sizes vary, and it's up to you which you use. The shells are removed before using in the recipes. If necessary, remove the vein running down the back of larger prawns and scampi with a sharp knife.

Cephalopods

Members of this family that are suitable for using in Balti recipes are octopus and squid.

BUYING FISH AND SHELLFISH

When buying fresh fish, check carefully that the eyes are clear and bright, not sunken. The fins should not be flabby. The gills should be firm and hard to open. The scales should all be in place, and the skin should look shiny and moist. There should not be an unpleasant smell.

White fish fillets should be neat and trim, and a white translucent colour. Avoid any with a blue tinge.

Bivalve shellfish should be firmly closed, or snap shut when tapped. If they gape open, they are probably dead, and should not be bought.

The fishmonger will clean, skin and fillet fish. He will also clean, scale and trim whole fish, removing head, fins and tail. He will be able to open shellfish like oysters and scallops for you, although it is better to do this at home, in order to catch their juices to use in cooking.

If you buy frozen fish, it should be hard, with no sign of partial thawing. The packaging should not be damaged.

Fresh fish and shellfish can be frozen at home providing it has not been frozen before. Interleave the fish or fillets with cling film. Thaw in a covered container in the bottom of the refrigerator, allowing a minimum of 12 hours. Do not thaw in water as there will be loss of texture, flavour and valuable nutrients.

COOKING FISH AND SHELLFISH

I prefer to cook fish steaks and fillets whole, as smaller pieces will tend to break up during the stir-frying. The fish can be cut up into bite-sized pieces just before serving, if you don't wish to serve them whole.

Be gentle when stir-frying fish.

BALTI FISH, MEDIUM HEAT

— ◆ —

This is a 'standard' medium-heat Balti preparation. It will result in bite-sized cubes of succulent fish in ample golden-brown gravy, neither too hot, nor too mild.

***Serves 4** (makes 4 portions)*

1¹/₂ lb (675 g) fish, fillets or steaks (any type)

2–3 tablespoons ghee or corn oil
3–6 garlic cloves, finely chopped
8 oz (225 g) onion, very finely chopped
3–4 tablespoons Balti masala paste (see page 38)

6 fl oz (175 ml) milk
1 teaspoon Balti garam masala (see page 33)
1 tablespoon very finely chopped fresh coriander leaves
aromatic salt to taste (see page 34)

1 Heat the ghee or oil in your karahi on high heat, then stir-fry the garlic for 30 seconds.

2 Add the onion on a reduced heat, and stir-fry for about 10 minutes, allowing the onion to become translucent and begin to brown.

3 Add the masala paste and the fish. Raise the heat again and bring to a brisk sizzle, stir-frying as needed for about 5 minutes.

4 Add the milk bit by bit and simmer, stirring, on a lower heat for about 10 minutes.

5 Test that the fish is cooked right through by removing a piece and cutting it in two. (Replace the halves in the pan.) If more cooking is needed, keep testing. When it is as you like it, add the garam masala, fresh coriander leaves and aromatic salt to taste.

BALTI LAKE FISH (SATPARA NYASHA)
— ◆ —

In the Satpara, a lake near the capital of Baltistan, a type of carp abound that would traditionally be used in this dish. Use any freshwater fish (except salmon) in this recipe. Marinate it first, then stir-fry Balti style.

Serves 4 *(makes 4 portions)*

1¹/₂ lb (675 g) freshwater fish
 (see page 77) (any type),
 weighed after filleting and
 skinning

2 tablespoons sesame oil
1 teaspoon sesame seeds
¹/₂ teaspoon green cardamom
 seeds
¹/₂ teaspoon black cummin seeds
¹/₂ teaspoon fenugreek seeds
¹/₂ teaspoon aniseed
2 teaspoons Balti masala mix
 (see page 31)
2 in (5 cm) cube fresh ginger,
 thinly sliced
6 oz (175 g) onion, thinly sliced
6 fl oz (175 ml) milk
25–30 saffron strands
1 tablespoon chopped fresh
 coriander leaves

2–3 tablespoons pistachio nuts,
 chopped
2 teaspoons granulated sugar
aromatic salt to taste (see page
 34)
1 tablespoon coriander seeds,
 roasted and lightly crushed
any green herbs for garnishing

MARINADE
6 garlic cloves, chopped
2 oz (50 g) onion, chopped
3 tablespoons coconut milk
 powder
1 tablespoon gram flour
1 tablespoon vegetable oil
0–4 red chillies, chopped
 (optional)
2 teaspoons paprika
1 tablespoon tomato purée

1 Grind together the marinade ingredients in a blender, food
processor or in the old-fashioned mortar and pestle with enough
water to achieve a thick but pourable paste.

2 Immerse the fish in the marinade in a non-metallic bowl, cover
and put into the fridge for 2–3 hours.

3 Heat the oil in the karahi, and stir-fry the seeds for 30 seconds.
Add the masala mix, ginger and onion, and stir-fry at a sizzle
for 3–4 minutes.

4 Add the milk. When simmering, add the fish and marinade.

5 Simmer for 10–15 minutes, adding a little extra milk or water if
it starts sticking.

6 Add the saffron, coriander leaves, nuts, sugar and aromatic salt
and simmer for a final 5 minutes or until the fish is cooked.

7 Garnish with the coriander seeds and green herbs. Serve with
plain rice.

BALTI KASHMIRI FISH

— ◆ —

A gorgeously spiced recipe from Pakistani Kashmir. The aromatic spices, yoghurt, and nuts make for a superb authentically-flavoured fish dish with a luscious gravy. The marinade prepares the fish for its short cooking. Serve fresh with bread and chutney.

Serves 4 *(makes 4 portions)*

1¹/₂ lb (675 g) fish fillets or steaks (any type), cut into manageable pieces

7 fl oz (200 ml) milk
¹/₂ teaspoon turmeric
1 tablespoon ghee or sesame oil
1 teaspoon cummin seeds
¹/₂ teaspoon coriander seeds
¹/₂ teaspoon fennel seeds

¹/₂ teaspoon lovage seeds
2 in (5 cm) cube fresh ginger, finely chopped
4 oz (110 g) Greek yoghurt aromatic salt to taste (see page 34)
20–30 cashew nuts, fried and roughly chopped
1 tablespoon chopped fresh herbs (coriander, parsley or basil)

1 Add the milk to the turmeric and soak the fish in it for 1¹/₂—2 hours.

2 Heat the ghee or oil in the karahi and stir-fry the seeds for 30 seconds. Add the ginger and continue for 30 more seconds.

3 Add the yoghurt then, once simmering, add the fish with its marinade.

4 Gently simmer, stirring, for about 10–15 minutes, or until the fish is cooked right through.

5 Add aromatic salt to taste. Garnish with the nuts and fresh herbs.

BALTI SMOKED FISH (KAMPO)

— ◆ —

Curing fish has been practised for thousands of years in regions where the winters make access to fresh fish impossible. The Balti people are no exception in their mountainous regions, and the fish they dry in the summer can be used at any time of year. Smoked haddock, though not authentic to the region, makes a fine Balti dish.

Serves 4 (*makes 4 portions*)

1½ lb (675 g) smoked haddock, weighed after filleting and skinning, cut into large pieces

2–3 tablespoons ghee or corn oil
3–6 garlic cloves, finely chopped
8 oz (225 g) onion, very finely chopped
3–4 tablespoons Balti masala paste (see page 38)
6 fl oz (175 ml) milk
3 fl oz (85 ml) single cream

1 tablespoon granulated sugar
1 teaspoon Balti garam masala (see page 33)
1 tablespoon very finely chopped fresh coriander leaves
aromatic salt to taste (see page 34)

SPICES
½ teaspoon lovage seeds
¼ teaspoon wild onion seeds

1 Heat the ghee or oil in your karahi on high heat, then stir-fry the garlic and **Spices** for 30 seconds.

2 Add the onion on a reduced heat, and stir-fry for about 10 minutes, allowing the onion to become translucent and begin to brown.

3 Add the masala paste, the milk and the smoked haddock. Raise the heat again and bring to a brisk sizzle, stir-frying as needed for about 5 minutes.

4 Add the cream and sugar and simmer, stirring, on a lower heat for about 10 minutes.

5 Test that the fish is cooked right through (see stage 5 on page 80). When as you like it, add the garam masala, fresh coriander leaves and aromatic salt to taste.

BALTI GRILLED FISH (TAPA)

— ♦ —

I find oily fish are always best grilled or deep-fried. This recipe is so simple: simply smear the whole fish with this savoury paste, then grill and serve with Balti Dip, Balti Salad and Balti Naan bread (pages 144 and 146–7) for an amazingly filling meal or snack.

Serves 4 *(makes 4 portions)*

4 *whole pilchards or herrings, about 10 in (25 cm) long, or 16 sardines, about 4 in (10 cm) long, cleaned*

SAVOURY PASTE
6 *tablespoons Balti masala paste (see page 38)*
2 *garlic cloves, finely chopped*
1 *in (2.5 cm) cube fresh ginger, finely chopped*
4 *oz (110 g) onion, finely chopped*
2 *tablespoons melted ghee or butter*

2 *teaspoons dried mint*
2 *teaspoons aromatic salt (see page 34)*
1 *tablespoon ground almonds*
4 *tablespoons Greek yoghurt*

GARNISH
Balti garam masala (see page 33)
aromatic salt (see page 34)
chilli powder (optional)
chopped pistachio nuts (optional)

1 Grind together the savoury paste ingredients in a blender, food processor or the old-fashioned mortar and pestle with enough water to achieve a thick but pourable paste.

2 Preheat the grill to medium hot. Line the grill tray with kitchen foil (to catch drips and make cleaning up easier). Put the grill rack into the tray. Put the fish on to the rack, close together.

3 Coat the top side of the fishes with half of the marinade.

4 Place the tray at the midway position and grill for 5–8 minutes (depending on fish and size and actual heat level). The fish should by then be cooking but not burned.

5 Remove the tray. Turn the fish, keeping them close together, and coat the otherside with the remaining marinade. Repeat the grilling (stage 4).

6 Sprinkle with garam masala, aromatic salt and chilli powder to taste and serve piping hot. If liked, garnish with chopped pistachio nuts.

BALTI FRIED BATTERED FISH (NAGOPA)
— ♦ —

Battered fish has been known in the sub-continent since before the Druids built Stonehenge. As you might suspect, Balti batter is a more complex mixture than ours, but it is supremely tasty.

Serves 4 *(makes 4 portions)*

8 *small white fish fillets (any type), each about 3 oz (75 g)*
3–4 tablespoons ghee.

lemon wedges

BATTER
5 oz (150 g) gram flour
1 oz (25 g) coconut milk powder
2 garlic cloves, finely chopped
1 tablespoon vinegar (any type)
3 tablespoons Greek yoghurt

1 tablespoon Balti garam masala (see page 33)
2 tablespoons Balti masala paste (see page 38)
2 teaspoons salt
2 teaspoons sugar
1 teaspoon white cummin seeds
¹/₂ teaspoon lovage seeds
0–4 fresh green chillies, finely chopped (optional)

1 Wash the fish fillets and pat them dry.

2 Mix the batter ingredients together, and add enough water to achieve a thickish, pourable paste.

3 Immerse the fish fillets in the batter in a large bowl. Cover and refrigerate for 1–2 hours.

4 Heat the ghee in a large flat frying pan. You will probably only be able to fit two or four fillets in at a time.

5 Fry for 5–8 minutes then turn and fry the other side for the same time. Serve whilst still crisp, with lemon wedges, dhal and plain rice.

BALTI PRAWNS

— ◆ —

Prawns remain very popular at the Balti house. They are, of course, stunningly quick and easy to stir-fry, so are the perfect Balti subject. You can use raw or cooked prawns of any size. The cooking times given in the method will vary accordingly.

Serves 4 *(makes 4 portions)*

1½ lb (675 g) prawns, any size

2–3 tablespoons ghee or corn oil
3 garlic cloves, thinly sliced
8 oz (25 g) onion, thinly sliced
3 tablespoons Balti masala paste (see page 38)
1 tablespoon tomato purée

0–4 fresh red or green chillies, chopped or sliced (optional)
1 red or green pepper, cut into small diamonds
2 teaspoons Balti garam masala (see page 33)
1 teaspoon paprika
salt to taste

1 Prepare the prawns as required (thaw, shell, wash, de-vein etc).

2 Heat the ghee in the karahi on high heat, and stir-fry the garlic for 30 seconds.

3 Add the onion on a reduced heat, and stir-fry for about 10 minutes, allowing the onion to become translucent and begin to brown.

4 Add the masala paste and the tomato purée and mix in well. Add the prawns, chillies and pepper. Raise the heat and bring to a brisk sizzle, stir-frying as needed for about 5–8 minutes.

5 Add the garam masala, paprika and salt to taste, plus splashes of water to prevent sticking. The end result should be quite dry.

6 Stir-fry for a further 5 minutes or until the prawns are fully cooked. Serve with breads and/or rice.

BALTI SCALLOPS

— ◆ —

This recipe is slightly unusual because it starts by cooking the main ingredient first, with the spices and flavourings being built up around it. It suits the Balti technique admirably, and can be used for any shellfish. I've used scallops here.

Serves 4 *(makes 4 portions)*

$1^1/_2$ *lb (675 g) shelled scallops, with their roe*

3–4 tablespoons ghee or oil
1 teaspoon white cummin seeds
6 cloves garlic, finely chopped
4 tablespoons dehydrated onion
1 tablespoon vinegar (any type)
1 tablespoon tomato ketchup

2 tablespoons Balti masala paste (see page 38)
6 fl oz (175 ml) tinned coconut milk
2 teaspoons Balti garam masala (see page 33)
salt to taste
10–12 fresh whole coriander and/or basil leaves to garnish

1 Heat the ghee or oil in the karahi. Add the scallops and the seeds, and stir-fry for about 2 minutes to seal the scallops.

2 Add the garlic, and stir-fry for a further 30 seconds.

3 At 1-minute intervals stir-fry in the following ingredients: the dehydrated onions with the vinegar, the tomato ketchup, the masala paste, and the coconut milk.

4 Lower the heat to achieve a minimal simmer, add the garam masala and salt to taste, and stir for a further 5–8 minutes or until the scallops are cooked. The dish should be relatively dry (but add a little water during the cooking as needed).

BALTI LOBSTER (OR MONKFISH)

— ◆ —

The flesh of a whole lobster is succulent and a real treat, but extremely expensive. To obtain sufficient flesh to serve four, you'll need to purchase two lobsters weighing around $2^3/_4$ lb (1.2 kg) each. A remarkable lobster substitute at a fraction of the price is monkfish.

To serve four, use $1^1/_2$ lb (675 g) lobster flesh (or monkfish fillets), diced into bite-sized pieces and use instead of the prawns or scallops in either of the previous two recipes.

BALTI OYSTER

— ◆ —

They serve Balti oysters at West Bromwich's **Memsahib Balti Bistro**, although I'm pretty sure they don't get them from Baltistan. It's novel and different, and worth trying.

Serves 4 *(makes 4 portions)*

24–30 fresh oysters, shelled
ghee or oil

$^1/_2$ teaspoon lovage seeds
$^1/_2$ teaspoon aniseed
$^1/_2$ teaspoon turmeric

2–4 garlic cloves, sliced
1 tablespoon Balti garam
   masala (see page 33)
1 tablespoon chopped fresh
   coriander leaves
lime wedges

1 Heat the ghee or oil in the karahi or wok. Fry the seeds and turmeric for 15–20 seconds, then add the garlic.

2 Add a cupful of water, and when this is simmering, add the oysters. Stir-fry for 7–8 minutes.

3 Add the garam masala and fresh coriander. Serve at once, with lime wedges for squeezing.

Opposite, top to bottom: a combination dish of Balti Chickpeas (pages 103–4) with mushrooms and green chillies (pages 94–5 and 97); Green Balti Roti (page 143); and a combination dish of okra and cherry tomatoes (pages 97 and 99–100) in a Spice Base for Vegetables made with green masala paste (pages 90–1)

CHAPTER · 5

Vegetables and Legumes

Baltistanis are definitely not vegetarians and they would never serve a meal without meat, poultry or fish. There is no reason, however, why you can't serve vegetable-only Balti dishes. You can still mix and match, in true Balti style, to create your own interesting combinations such as aubergine and carrot with mushroom, or dhal with broccoli.

Like the Baltistanis, the Balti restaurants combine vegetables with meat, poultry or fish to make one complete dish: meat with sweetcorn and potato, chicken with celery, fish with lobia beans are three typical combinations. It is exactly this mix-and-match facility which has made the UK Balti house so popular. As I've already mentioned in the Introduction, more than one restaurant has multiple-choice dishes so long on their menus that they appear in an abbreviated code, well understood by Baltimaniacs. 'Balti meat-veg-dal-spi-chana' appears, exactly as written here, on the menu at **Adil Balti House** in Sparkbrook, Birmingham!

In this chapter I have looked at vegetables individually, vegetable by vegetable, and given single-portion recipes which serve one person. If you want to make more portions, simply double or quadruple all quantities as required.

Lentils require rather more time-consuming preparation and cooking, but as they are used a lot in Balti combinations, I've provided ten-portion recipes, with the idea that you use what's needed and freeze the rest to use later. Instructions for cooking legumes begin on page 100.

Opposite, top to bottom: Balti Patia (page 121), Balti Special Chutney (page 146), and Balti Dhansak (page 111)

VEGETABLE-ONLY BALTI DISHES

The idea is to select your vegetables and prepare and cook them as instructed in the A-Z of Vegetables, and then combine them with the Balti Spice Base. The recipe for this and its variations starts below. You can combine any vegetables with any variation of the spice base – the choice is yours.

For *each person* you will need 6 oz (175 g) raw vegetables (weighed after peeling etc) and 1 portion of Balti Spice Base.

COMBINATION DISHES

If you want to substitute vegetables for part of the meat, poultry or fish quantity in any of the Balti recipes in this book, then simply prepare the vegetables as instructed in the A-Z of Vegetables and add to your chosen Balti dish just before serving (unless otherwise instructed). It's up to you how many items you mix and match.

To help you work out quantities, all recipes in the book state how many **portions** they make. If, for example, you wanted to make a combination dish of Balti Meat, Medium Heat (page 46) and broccoli, you could combine 2 portions (ie half the given recipe) of Balti Meat Medium Heat with 2 portions of cooked broccoli (ie 2 x 6 oz/175 g uncooked weight of broccoli) to give you a Balti combination dish that will serve 4 people.

THREE BALTI SPICE BASES FOR VEGETABLES

— ◆ —

The following recipe can be made with Balti, green or tandoori masala paste, to give three variations. Each of these variations can be varied again by adding your choice of optional extras from those suggested at the end of the recipe. This gives more than 21 different spice base possibilities, all formulated to go well with all the vegetables which appear in this chapter – it's up to you to mix and match as the mood takes you. Each is a single portion base but can be made in bulk (say ten or more portions) by simply scaling up the quantities. You can then divide the base into yoghurt pots and freeze.

The beauty of this single-portion recipe is that it is fast to cook.

Serves 1 *(makes a single portion)*

2 teaspoons light sunflower or
  soya oil
1 garlic clove, thinly sliced
2 oz (50 g) onion, chunkily
  sliced

1 tablespoon of either Balti
  masala paste, green masala
  paste or tandoori masala
  paste (see pages 38 and 39)

1 Heat the oil in the karahi, then stir-fry the garlic for about 15 seconds. Add the onion and stir-fry for around 1 minute.

2 Add the paste of choice and stir-fry for a further 2 minutes.

3 Remove from the heat and cool and freeze **or** add 1 portion of the vegetable of your choice from pages 93–100 and stir-fry to heat through, **or** use as directed in a specific recipe.

SPICE BASE OPTIONAL EXTRAS
— ♦ —

There are some simple 'add-on' flavourings which can be incorporated into the previous Balti spice base for vegetables. Choose from the following:

Serves 1 *(one portion)*

Acidic: 1¹/₂ teapoons tomato purée and the juice of 1 lemon
Exotic: 2 teaspoons desiccated coconut
Hot: 1 or more teaspoons chilli powder
Rich: 3 tablespoons single cream
Savoury: 2 teaspoons dry fenugreek leaves and 1 teaspoon water
Sour: 2–3 tablespoons Greek yoghurt
Sweet: 1 teaspoon granulated sugar

Follow the base recipe above, and add one or more optional extra(s) at the end of stage 2.

COOKING VEGETABLES FOR BALTI

— ◆ —

There are three generalised methods for cooking vegetables for Balti – by boiling, by steaming or by microwaving. For tips on preparing specific vegetables, see pages 93–100.

Serves 1 *(single portion)*

6 oz (175 g) vegetables of your
*   choice, weighed after the*
*   appropriate trimming,*
*   peeling etc.*

Method 1: BOILING

1 Boil ³/₄ pint (450 ml) water in a saucepan.

2 Dice the vegetables into bite-sized pieces.

3 Boil for 3–4 minutes, or until as you like it. Some vegetables, such as potatoes, turnips and parsnips, may take longer.

4 Strain and use as required.

Method 2: STEAMING

You can use Chinese bamboo tiered steamers held above a saucepan containing boiling water, a double boiler or, cheapest of all, a strainer simply placed above the pan.

1 Boil ¹/₂ pint (300 ml) of water in a saucepan or double-boiler base.

2 Dice the vegetables into bite-sized pieces.

3 Put the vegetables into the steamer tray, upper half of the double boiler or the strainer. Place over the boiling water, put the lid on and steam until just tender – or cooked to your liking.

Method 3: MICROWAVING

This is one of the best uses of a microwave. In no time at all, the vegetable is piping hot, yet minimal flavour is lost due to minimal water being involved in the cooking process.

1 Dice the vegetables into bite-sized pieces

2 Place 2 fl oz (50 ml) cold water and the vegetables into a suitably sized, wide-lidded non-metallic bowl.

3 Run the microwave for $1^{1}/_{2}$ minutes. Test and continue until the vegetables are as you want them. A little more water may be needed if it dries out.

A-Z OF VEGETABLES

Note: When recipes call for 1 portion of a particular vegetable, this means 6 oz/175 g (weighed before cooking but after peeling etc).

Aubergine

An oblong, pear- or egg-shaped, fleshy berry fruit, generally deep purple, from $2^{1}/_{2}$–12 in (6–30 cm) long.

Wash, then halve and discard the central pith and seeds. Dice into bite-sized pieces, retaining the skin. Boil, steam or microwave to tender. Add to your chosen Balti recipe, or flavour with a Balti Spice Base of your choice (see pages 90–1).

Broccoli or Calabrese

A type of brassica with short fleshy green buds, clustered in a single head.

Wash, and remove leaves and bottom of stalk. Cut into small florets, and cut the stalk into small chunks. Boil, steam or microwave to tender. Add to your chosen Balti recipe or flavour with a Balti Spice Base of your choice (see pages 90–1).

Carrots

A long cylindrical tapering root, bright orange in colour. It can be eaten raw, so needs minimal cooking.

Discard tops and tails, wash then pare and cut into strips, rounds or cubes. Boil, steam or microwave to tender. Add to your chosen Balti recipe or flavour with a Balti Spice Base of your choice (see pages 90–1).

Cauliflower

Originating in the Middle East, this brassica is made up of short stems holding a number of florets, which are normally white, but can be green, yellow or red.

Wash and cut off leaves and bottom of stalk. Cut into small florets, and cut the stalk into small chunks. Boil, steam or microwave to tender. Add to your chosen Balti recipe or flavour with a Balti Spice Base of your choice (see pages 90–1).

Celery

An herbaceous plant with long white or green, fleshy, slightly stringy stems. These can be eaten raw, so minimal cooking is needed.

Cut off the pithy base, and the leaves, wash then cut the sticks into bite-sized pieces. Boil, steam or microwave to tender. Add to your chosen Balti recipe or flavour with a Balti Spice Base of your choice (see pages 90–1).

Chilli

The hot member of the capsicum family. Of the many species of chillies, the best are the long thin cylindrical tapering fruit, measuring 2–4 in (5–10 cm). All chillies are green, and ripen to red. The heat aspect from chillies is called capsaicin, and is most intense in the seeds.

Chilli heat tolerance levels vary from person to person from nil to unlimited. On average one hottish chilli per single portion is enough. Wash it, de-stalk it, and chop it into narrow rings or slices, or keep it whole. You may discard the seeds, but that's a bit like throwing the baby out with the bath water! It is the seeds which provide the heat and contrary to some misinformation, they do not cause indigestion to those used to them.

Chilli needs no prior boiling, steaming or microwaving. Simply add to the recipe of your choice at the stage after the spices, garlic and onion are fried, or as individual recipes direct.

CHEF'S TIP

Freeze spare whole chillies unblanched for use as required.

Green Beans

Runner beans, snap beans, French or Kenyan beans are all fleshy pods, usually green, but sometimes purple or yellow. The largest are runners growing up to 10 in (25 cm) in length. The smallest, the snap bean, is about 4 in (10 cm) in length.

Top, tail (and, in the case of runners, pull off the scaly strings), then cut into strips or crosswise. Boil, steam or microwave to tender. Add to your chosen Balti recipe or flavour with a Balti Spice Base of your choice (see pages 90–1).

Karela

A knobbly, long, cylindrical, pointed green gourd, native to the sub-continent but widely available in the West. It is very bitter, and an acquired taste.

Wash, discard the top and tail, and dice into bite-sized pieces. Boil, steam or microwave to tender. Add to your chosen Balti recipe or flavour with a Balti Spice Base of your choice (see pages 90–1).

Lotus Root

A rather extraordinary perforated root, indigenous to and very popular in Baltistan and Kashmir, and available at specialist Asian greengrocers in the UK.

Peel off the skin, wash and cut as required. Boil, steam or microwave to tender. Add to your chosen Balti recipe or flavour with a Balti Spice Base of your choice (see pages 90–1).

Mangetout

The fleshy pods and tiny seeds of a member of the pea family (hence its alternative names, snow pea or sugar pea). The whole thing is eaten after topping and tailing. It can be eaten raw, but being flat and relatively small, it makes a perfect Balti stir-fry subject. Alternatively, boil steam or microwave to tender.

The following recipe is complete, and does not require a Spice Base.

BALTI MANGETOUT
— ◆ —

Serves 1 *(single portion)*

6 oz (175 g) mangetouts, topped
 and tailed
2 tablespoons sunflower or light
 oil
¹/₂ teaspoon panch phoran (see
 page 35)

1 teaspoon granulated sugar
1 tablespoon chopped fresh
 coriander leaves
aromatic salt to taste (see page
 34)

1 Heat the oil in the karahi, and stir-fry the panch phoran for 20 seconds.

2 Add the mangetouts and after a short sizzle, lower the heat. Add splashes of water and stir regularly.

3 After about 5 minutes, add the sugar, the fresh coriander and salt to taste. Once these have amalgamated, serve promptly.

Marrow

A member of the gourd family growing to quite huge dimensions, but averaging 12 in (30 cm). Its water content is high, so requires minimal cooking.

Halve, remove the central seedy mush and the hard skin, and cut the flesh into bite-sized pieces. Boil, steam or microwave to tender. Add to your chosen Balti recipe or flavour with a Balti Spice Base of your choice (see pages 90–1).

Mushrooms

There are literally hundreds of species of these edible fungi to choose from. The most familiar are mass cultivated and include field, cup, button and flat. Other less familiar cultivated varieties include beefsteak fungus, parasol, cep, blewit, pleurotte and oyster. All have distinctive flavours, but are handled in the same way.

Peel only if they really need it then wash and pat dry. Add raw to the Balti recipe of your choice towards the end of the cooking time. (Mushrooms *can* stand long cooking, but are best for flavour after just a few minutes.)

To make one portion of **Balti Mushrooms**, stir-fry 6 oz (175 g) mushrooms in 1 tablespoon ghee or oil for 2–3 minutes, then flavour with a Balti Spice Base of your choice (see pages 90–1).

Okra

A green, cylindrical seed capsule, with a pointed tip and longitudinal grooves. The sizes range from about $2^1/_2$ in (6 cm) to as much as 10 in (25 cm). Select soft not scaly specimens, no more than $4^1/_2$ in (11 cm) long. Okra, also known as bindi or ladies' fingers, can be eaten raw. Once cut they ooze sap, so cut just before cooking and eat at once.

The microwave provides excellent results, steaming is all right, but boiling creates sap. Best of all, in my view, is a stir-fry.

To stir-fry, wash 8 oz (225 g) okra thoroughly and put aside until just before you need to cook it. Cut off the stalk (and tip if necessary) and cut the okra into $^3/_4$ inch (2 cm) pieces at the last possible minute. Stir-fry in 1 tablespoon of ghee or vegetable oil until cooked to your liking. Flavour at once with a Balti Spice Base of your choice (pages 90–1) or add immediately to your chosen Balti dish.

Parsnip

As *Potato*

Peas

Small green spheres which grow in an inedible pod. Most of the crop are taken by frozen food factories, and peas are one of their better products. Fresh peas are available in season, and they make a refreshing change from the ubiquitous frozen items.

Whether using fresh or frozen peas, boil, steam or microwave to tender. Add to your chosen Balti recipe or flavour with a Balti Spice Base (see pages 90–1).

If you intend to add peas to other Balti curries, do so towards the end of cooking so that you retain their wonderful green colour.

Peppers

Also known as bell peppers, sweet peppers, paprika, pimentos and the capsicum. In fact they're just one member of the massive capsicum family to which chillies also belong. Red and green peppers are the most common, and they also come in white, yellow, orange and purple. They are very mild in flavour. They are a roughly heart-shaped, fleshy, hollow fruit berry, measuring up to $4^{1}/_{2}$ (11 cm) in length. Half a pepper is enough for one portion.

Cut off the stem end, remove seeds, and cut into chosen shapes and sizes (dice, chunks, strips etc.).

They are attractive to use in Balti dishes, giving good colour contrasts. The red, orange and yellow stand up to prolonged cooking better than do green, which tends to go rather grey (but still taste good) if cooked for some time. To counter this, you can blanch, steam or microwave the pre-cut pepper, softening it and heating it sufficiently to enable it to be added at a relatively late stage of cooking. Alternatively omit the softening stage, and add it after the fry-up of the spices, garlic, onion and masala paste stages in your chosen Balti curry.

To make Balti peppers, simply stir-fry in your chosen Balti Spice Base (see pages 90–1).

Potato

It is hard to believe that the world's most popular vegetable was not known in Europe before Francis Drake's voyage back from Virginia in 1584. The potato is a tuber, round or oval, varying in size from $^{1}/_{2}$ inch (1 cm) to 4 in (10 cm) in diameter. No other vegetable is as versatile as the potato, which can be boiled, baked, roasted, fried or mashed.

Scrub clean, and peel old potatoes only. Dice large ones into roughly equal bite-sized cubes; small ones can be halved or left whole. Boil, steam or microwave to tender, for around 10–15 minutes depending on the potato type and size of piece. Alternatively deep fry the chunks. Add to your chosen Balti recipe or flavour with a Balti Spice Base of your choice (pages 90–1).

Spinach

The dark green leaf of an herbaceous plant, this delicious vegetable gets its unique flavour from its oxalic acid content. Thought to have originated in Iran, it is very popular in the sub-continent. It is also high in iron.

Remove the thick stalks. Boil, steam or microwave to tender. Add to your chosen Balti recipes or flavour with a Balti Spice Base of your choice (pages 90–1).

Sweet Potato and Yam

Sweet potatoes, whether red or white, are not related to ordinary potatoes. They are fleshy, thick roots, the skin colour varying from light yellow to reddish-violet. The flesh of red sweet potato is orange and sweet, and that of the white sweet potato is yellow, drier and less sweet.

The yam is an unrelated tuberous root, high in starch, with a crinkled brown skin and white flesh which is not so sweet.

Sizes are similar to those of large potatoes. Cook as potatoes.

Sweetcorn

Sweetcorn is a form of maize, a tall grass, and the familiar golden cobs yield hundeds of soft tasty grains. They can be eaten raw but light short boiling converts the starch to sugar.

Remove leaves and strings from the cobs, then cut the grains off the cob. Boil, steam or microwave to tender. Add to your chosen Balti recipe or flavour with a Balti Spice Base of your choice (pages 90–1).

Tomatoes

A juicy fruit which is normally round, though some species grow in oval or pear shapes. When ripe they are usually scarlet, though some orange varieties are available. For decades flavour has been sacrificed for quantity by the larger growers, although recently things have started to improve. In addition there are new and tastier types available, such as plum, beefsteak and cherry tomatoes. Canned tomatoes (normally plum tomatoes) can be substituted.

Tomatoes are not usually served alone, although I don't know why not. Tomato needs no pre-cooking.

Remove stalks and wash, if fresh, or strain canned tomatoes. Simply chop up and add to your chosen Balti recipe virtually at any stage after the initial fry-up of the spices, garlic, onion and masala paste.

If added to a Baltic Spice Base, stir-fry with the paste in stage 2 of the recipe on page 91.

Turnip

As *Potato*

LEGUMES

Lentils, dried beans and peas are legumes, and their seeds – also called pulses – have been dried since mankind first began civilised farming. In the dried form they lasted for years, and traditionally provided protein over hard winters and non-growing periods. Balti people have long since relied on legumes, and they are an important ingredient in Balti dishes.

As with vegetables, they can be used in a mix-and-match combination method.

In this section, I give recipes for more than one portion, because it is impractical to cook legumes in tiny batches. In fact it is far easier to cook a whole 500 g (18 oz) packet in one go, and store the spare in the freezer. 500 g (18 oz) yields enough for around ten to twelve portions, so use large yoghurt pots to freeze the excess in.

CHEF'S TIP

Lentils and beans are available in tins, the nett weight of contents usually being 14 oz (400 g) including liquid. The liquid can be used in stock. You can save considerable time using tinned lentils, although it costs a little more than the home-cooked equivalent.

COOKING LEGUMES
— ♦ —

1 Spread the legumes out on a table and examine them carefully. Small stones, even large pieces of grit, are not uncommon, because the villagers still dry legumes on the ground.

2 For the same reason a good cold water rinse/wash is essential.

3 Soak the legumes. Timings vary from species to species. The reason is to leach out starch (and toxins, in some cases) and to soften the legumes in order to shorten their cooking time.

4 Cooking can be in water in a saucepan or in the microwave. As they take in water, the legumes will expand to $1^1/_2$ to 2 times their dry size. Use a saucepan large enough to allow for this. Cooking times too vary from species to species, so follow the instructions on the packet.

BALTI MASOOR LENTILS
— ♦ —

Masoor Dhal

There are many small lentils which make excellent dhal. The most readily available and the fastest to cook is the red lentil in its split and polished form.

Serves 10 *(makes 10 portions)*

18 oz (500 g) packet of split and polished red lentils (masoor)
4 tablespoons Balti masala paste (see page 38)

8 tablespoons fried dehydrated onion flakes (see page 28)
2 garlic cloves, finely chopped aromatic salt to taste (see page 34)

1 Examine and rinse the lentils as described above. Soak in cold water for around 30–45 minutes. Strain and rinse.

101

2 Bring twice the volume of water of the soaked lentils to the boil.

3 Give the lentils a final hot rinse and place them in the boiling water. Stir after a few minutes to ensure the lentils are not sticking.

4 Reduce the heat to achieve a gentle simmer. Leave the lentils to cook for about 30 minutes, stirring from time to time and skimming off any scum as it forms. Keep an eye on the water content. It *should* absorb precisely. If it looks too dry add some water.

5 Add the remaining ingredients, including aromatic salt to taste, and simmer for a minimum of ten minutes.

6 Serve on its own or added to other Balti recipes. Freeze any surplus.

BALTI GRAM LENTILS
— ◆ —
Chana Dhal

An important lentil which orginated in the Himalayas and is widely used in Balti cooking. It resembles the yellow split pea in colour and size, and it is this lentil which is used to make gram flour (*besan*).

Serves 10 (makes 10 portions)

18 oz (500 g) packet of split and polished gram lentils (chana)
4 tablespoons green masala paste (see page 39)

8 tablespoons fried dehydrated onion flakes (see page 28)
2 tablespoons granulated sugar (optional)
salt to taste

1 Examine and rinse the lentils as described on page 101. Soak in cold water for at least 6 hours. Strain and rinse.

2 Bring 4 pints (2.25 litres) water to the boil.

3 Add the lentils, stirring after a few minutes to ensure they are not sticking.

4 Reduce the heat to a gentle simmer. Leave to cook for about 45 minutes, skimming off any scum as it forms. When tender, strain (keeping the liquid for stock).

5 Add the remaining ingredients, including salt to taste, and simmer for a minimum of 10 minutes.

6 Serve on its own or added to other Balti recipes (for example Balti Chana Aloo, pages 130–1), or add vegetables of your choice (see A-Z of Vegetables). Freeze any surplus.

BALTI CHICKPEAS
— ♦ —
Kabli Chana

The largest member of the lentil family, the dried chickpea is a rock-hard sphere about $5/8$ in (1.5 cm) in diameter. After prolonged soaking it cooks to a firm yet tender texture, giving good colour and visual interest as well as a fine taste.

Serves 10 *(makes 10 portions)*

18 oz (500 g) packet of
  chickpeas (kabli chana)
4 tablespoons tandoori masala
  paste (see page 39)
8 tablespoons fried dehydrated
  onion flakes (see page 28)

1 tablespoon dried mint
  (optional)
6 tablespoons Greek yoghurt
salt

1 Examine and rinse the chickpeas as described on page 101. Soak in cold water for at least 12 hours. Strain and rinse.

2 Bring 4 pints (2.25 litres) water to the boil.

3 Add the chickpeas. When the water comes to the boil again, reduce to a simmer.

4 Leave to simmer for 45–60 minutes. Test that they are tender. Strain, discarding the liquid.

5 Add the remaining ingredients to the chickpeas, including salt to taste, and simmer for a minimum of 10 minutes. Serve on its own or added to other Balti recipes (such as Balti Veg-Spi-Dal-Chi, page 133), or add vegetables of your choice (see A-Z of Vegetables). Freeze any surplus.

BALTI LOBIA (BLACK-EYED) BEANS
— ♦ —

Also known as cowpeas, these white beans with a tiny black 'eye' are attractive and high in nutrients. As the use of beans is less frequent in Balti cooking than lentils, I have given a quantity for two portions here. It can easily be stepped up or down.

Serves 2 (*makes 2 portions*)

5 oz (150 g) black-eyed beans
3 oz (75 g) onion, thinly sliced
1 teaspoon Balti garam masala
   (see page 33)

salt to taste
0–2 teaspoons chilli powder
   (optional)

1 Examine and rinse the beans as described on page 101. Soak in cold water for at least 12 hours. Strain and rinse.

2 Bring 1 pint (600 ml) water to the boil.

3 Add the beans. When the water comes to the boil again, reduce to a simmer.

4 Leave the beans to simmer for 45–60 minutes. Test that they are tender. Strain, discarding the liquid.

5 Add the remaining ingredients to the beans, including salt to taste. Serve added to other Balti recipes (such as Balti Lobia Beans, Mushrooms and Spinach, page 132).

BALTI RED KIDNEY BEANS

— ♦ —

This immensely popular dry bean obtains its name from its shape and its reddish-purple colour. Particular attention must be paid to removing the toxins in the bean (see stage 3 below).

Serves 2 *(makes 2 portions)*

5 oz (150 g) red kidney beans
3 oz (75 g) onion, thinly sliced
1 teaspoon Balti garam masala
(see page 33)

0–2 teaspoons chilli powder
(optional)
salt

1 Examine and rinse the beans as described on page 101. Soak in cold water for at least 12 hours. Strain and rinse.

2 Bring 1 pint (600 ml) water to the boil.

3 Add the beans. When the water comes back to the boil, boil for 10 minutes. This destroys the toxins.

4 Leave the beans to simmer for 45–60 minutes. Test that they are tender. Strain, discarding the liquid.

5 Add the remaining ingredients to the beans, including salt to taste. Serve added to other Balti recipes.

PANEER (CHEESE)

Paneer is the solid 'cheese' made by separating the curds from the whey in milk, then compressing it. Although not a vegetable, I have included it in this chapter because it can be used in vegetable combination dishes, or served in one of the Balti Spice Bases for vegetables (pages 90–1).

BALTI PANEER

— ◆ —

Paneer is really easy to make and the whey that is left at the end can be used for soup or stock.

Makes about 6 oz (175 g) paneer

*3 pints (1.8 litres) full cream
  milk (not UHT)*

*3–4 tablespoons any vinegar or
  lemon juice*

1 Choose a large pan. If you have one of 9 pint (5 litres) capacity, the milk will only occupy a third of the pan and won't boil over (unless the lid is on).

2 Bring the milk slowly to the boil. Add the vinegar or lemon juice, stirring until it curdles – when the curds separate from the whey.

3 Strain into a clean tea towel placed on a strainer over a saucepan. Fold the tea towel over and press through the excess liquid – the whey. Keep for later use as stock.

4 Now place the curds – from now on called paneer – on to the draining board, still in the tea towel. Press it out to a circle about ¹/₂ inch (1 cm) thick. Place a flat weight (the original saucepan full of water, for instance) on the tea towel and allow it to compress the paneer.

5 If you want crumbly paneer, remove the weight after 30–45 minutes. Crumble the paneer and use as the recipe directs. If you want the paneer to be solid, keep the weight on for 1¹/₂-2 hours. Then cut the paneer into cubes.

You can use the paneer like this, or you can shallow fry it in ghee or oil in the karahi or wok until golden. Serve in a Balti Spice Base of your choice (see pages 90–1), or use as a main ingredient in one of the combination dishes in Chapter 7.

CHAPTER · 6

Balti Specials

The restaurateurs who started the Balti craze going in Birmingham quickly realised that they would need to offer a whole range of familiar restaurant curry favourite dishes in the Balti style. That way they would be sure that their customers would be satisfied that Balti was not too new and daunting an experience.

In this chapter, I am following the same logic, and here you will find favourite curries like Bhoona, Ceylon, Dhansak, Do-piaza, Exotica, Jal Frezi, Kashmiri, Kofta, Korma, Madras, Malaya, Moglai, Patia, Phal, Rhogan Josh and Vindaloo, all cooked in the Balti style.

For most of these recipes it's up to you what you use as the main ingredient. You can choose from par-cooked meat of any kind (par-cooked as in the recipe on page 45), raw boneless poultry, raw fish or shellfish, or any raw or cooked vegetables from Chapter 5. You could even use a combination of these ingredients.

The vegetables should be prepared as instructed in Chapter 5, which generally means cutting into bite-sized cubes.

Simmering times in the recipes in this chapter are vague, because they depend on what main ingredients you are using. I have simply said in each recipe method to 'simmer until cooked to your liking'. However, to give you a rough idea, par-cooked meat and raw poultry will take 15–20 minutes; raw fish and shellfish will take up to 15 minutes; raw vegetables will take up to 10 minutes, depending on size, and cooked or softened vegetables will take up to 5 minutes. Use your judgement, and keep testing pieces of the food to see if it is cooked to your liking. You'll soon get the idea.

SPECIAL BALTI BASE SAUCE

— ♦ —

This is a mild creamy Balti sauce needed to make the special recipes in this chapter. You can make it in bulk (it freezes well), by stepping up the quantities as required or make it as a one-off sauce. The total time involved is about 45 minutes, including preparation. But, as most of this time is simmering, you can do other things, such as par-cook meat ready for the next stage or generally prepare other dishes.

Makes about 15 fl oz (450 ml)

7 fl oz (200 ml) milk
7 fl oz (200 ml) water
2 tablespoons ghee or vegetable oil
3 garlic cloves, finely chopped
8 oz (225 g) onion, very finely chopped
4 oz (110 g) carrot, finely chopped
2 oz (50 g) celeriac, chopped
2 oz (50 g) white radish (mooli), chopped

SPICES
4 bay leaves
8–10 green cardamoms, split open
several pieces of cassia bark, about 4 in (10 cm) total length
1 teaspoon fennel seeds
$1/_2$ teaspoon turmeric
1 in (2.5 cm) cube fresh ginger, quartered

1 Bring the milk and water to the boil with the **Spices**. Simmer for 10–15 minutes. Remove from the heat and strain, discarding the spices.

2 Heat the ghee or oil in your karahi. Stir-fry the garlic for 30 seconds, add the onion and stir-fry for 5 minutes.

3 Add the spicy milk, the carrot, celeriac and white radish allow to simmer for 30 minutes or so. It should never go too dry, but neither should it be swimming in liquid.

4 Cool sufficiently to allow you to blend it to a fine purée in the blender. It should be easily pourable, so add a little water if needed.

BALTI BHOONA CURRY

— ♦ —

The bhoona is a fundamental cooking method involving the frying of the ingredients. Because minimal liquid is involved, the ultimate texture of the dish is quite dry. To achieve this we only use half the Special Balti Base Sauce given opposite, thereby considerably reducing the liquid content.

Serves 4 (makes 4 portions)

1¹/₂ *lb (675 g) main ingredient of your choice (par-cooked meat using the recipe on page 45, or raw poultry cubes, or raw fish or shellfish, or any vegetables from Chapter 5, or a combination of main ingredients)*

7 fl oz (225 ml) Special Balti Base Sauce (see page 108)

1 tablespoon ghee or vegetable oil

2–3 garlic cloves, finely chopped

2 tablespoons Balti masala paste (see page 38)

1 tablespoon ground almonds

2 teaspoons Balti garam masala (see page 33)

4 tablespoons fried dehydrated onion flakes (see page 28)

aromatic salt to taste (see page 34)

some fresh coriander leaves to garnish

SPICES (roasted and crushed)
1 teaspoon white cummin seeds
1 teaspoon coriander seeds
1 teaspoon sesame seeds

1 Heat the oil in the karahi. Stir-fry the **Spices** for 30 seconds then stir-fry the garlic for 30 seconds. Add and stir-fry the masala paste for a further minute.

2 Add the main ingredient or ingredients of your choice and briskly stir-fry for about 3 minutes.

3 Stir in the Special Balti Base Sauce and bring it to the simmer.

4 Add the ground almonds, garam masala, onion flakes and aromatic salt to taste and simmer until it is cooked to your liking. It should be quite dry but not sticking to the pan. Garnish with fresh coriander leaves and serve.

BALTI CEYLON CURRY

— ◆ —

The Special Balti Base Sauce is enlivened with lemon and chilli to give a tart hotness that is countered by the coconut. This Balti curry evokes the balmy palmy sunny land of Sri Lanka.

Serves 4 *(makes 4 portions)*

1¹/₂ lb (675 g) main ingredient of your choice (par-cooked meat using the recipe on page 45, or raw poultry cubes, or raw fish or shellfish, or any vegetables from Chapter 5, or a combination of main ingredients)

15 fl oz (450 ml) Special Balti Base Sauce (see page 108)
4 tablespoons water
1¹/₂ oz (40 g) creamed coconut block
2 tablespoons ghee or oil

2–3 garlic cloves, finely chopped
2 tablespoons tandoori masala paste (see page 39)
2 tablespoons desiccated coconut
juice of one lemon
0–2 fresh green chillies (optional)
aromatic salt to taste (see page 34)
desiccated coconut to garnish

SPICES
1 teaspoon cummin seeds
¹/₂ teaspoon fennel seeds

1 Heat the water in a saucepan. Add the creamed coconut block and allow to melt until creamy and bubbling.

2 Heat the ghee or oil in the karahi and stir-fry the **Spices** for 30 seconds. Add the garlic and stir-fry for a further 30 seconds.

3 Add the main ingredient or ingredients of your choice and briskly stir-fry for about 1 minute. Add and stir-fry the masala paste for a further minute.

4 Stir in the special Balti Base Sauce and bring it to the simmer.

5 Add the desiccated coconut, lemon juice, chillis and aromatic salt to taste. Simmer until it is cooked to your liking. Garnish with desiccated coconut and serve.

BALTI DHANSAK

— ♦ —

One of the all-time Balti favourites. The sauce is thickened with creamy cooked lentils.

Serves 4 *(makes 4 portions)*

1¹/₂ lb (675 g) main ingredient of your choice (par-cooked meat using the recipe on page 45, or raw poultry cubes, or raw fish or shellfish, or any vegetables from Chapter 5, or a combination of main ingredients)

15 fl oz (450 ml) Special Balti Base Sauce (see page 108)
1 tablespoon ghee or vegetable oil
2–3 garlic cloves, finely chopped
1¹/₂ tablespoons Balti masala paste (see page 38)

2 portions Balti Masoor Lentils (see page 101)
1 tablespoon granulated sugar
2 teaspoons vinegar (any type)
2 teaspoons Balti garam masala (see page 33)
0–3 fresh green chillies, finely chopped (optional)
aromatic salt to taste (see page 34)
some fresh coriander leaves or chopped red pepper to garnish

SPICES
1 teaspoon cummin seeds
¹/₂ teaspoon fenugreek seeds

1 Heat the ghee or oil in the karahi. Stir-fry the **Spices** for 30 seconds then add and stir-fry the garlic for a further 30 seconds. Add and stir-fry the masala paste for a further minute.

2 Add the main ingredient or ingredients of your choice and briskly stir-fry for about 3 minutes.

3 Add the Special Balti Base Sauce and bring it to the simmer.

4 Add the remaining ingredients and aromatic salt to taste. Simmer until it is cooked to your liking. Garnish with coriander or red pepper and serve.

BALTI DO-PIAZA

— ◆ —

Lashings of onions (*piaza*) and a little honey create a very savoury dish tempered by a hint of sweetness.

Serves 4 (*makes 4 portions*)

1¹/₂ lb (657 g) main ingredient of your choice (par-cooked meat using the recipe on page 45, or raw poultry cubes, or raw fish or shellfish, or any vegetables from Chapter 5, or any combination of main ingredients)

7¹/₂ fl oz (225 ml) Special Balti Base Sauce (see page 108)

1 tablespoon ghee or vegetable oil

1 teaspoon panch phoran (see page 34)

2–3 garlic cloves, finely chopped

1¹/₂ tablespoons Balti masala paste (see page 38)

4 oz (110 g) onion, thinly sliced

1 tablespoon clear honey

4 tablespoons dehydrated onion flakes

aromatic salt to taste (see page 34)

some fresh coriander leaves to garnish

1 Heat the ghee or oil in the karahi. Stir-fry the **panch phoran** for 30 seconds then add and stir-fry the garlic for a further 30 seconds. Add and stir-fry the masala paste for a further minute.

2 Add the main ingredient or ingredients of your choice and briskly stir-fry for about 3 minutes.

3 Stir in the Special Balti Base Sauce and bring to the simmer.

4 Add the remaining ingredients and aromatic salt to taste. Simmer until it is cooked to your looking. Garnish with coriander leaves and serve.

BALTI EXOTICA

— ♦ —

Dreamed up by one of the more adventurous Balti house owners, you can dream up your *own* tropical additives. My version here adds nuts, coconut, mango, banana and kiwi fruit to the Balti base special sauce to produce a fruity dish which is not too sweet.

Serves 4 *(makes 4 portions)*

$1^1/_2$ *lb (675 g) main ingredient of your choice (par-cooked meat using the recipe on page 45, or raw poultry cubes, or raw fish or shellfish, or any vegetables from Chapter 5, or any combination of main ingredients)*

15 fl oz (450 ml) Special Balti Base Sauce (see page 108)
1 tablespoon ghee or vegetable oil
2–3 garlic cloves, finely chopped

2 tablespoons tandoori masala paste (see page 39)
2 tablespoons shelled peanuts
3 tablespoons fresh coconut flesh, cut into chippings
1 fresh mango, cubed
2 firm bananas, cut into rings
aromatic salt to taste (see page 34)
some kiwi fruit, peeled and sliced, to garnish
some fresh coriander leaves to garnish

1 Heat the oil in the karahi and stir-fry the garlic for 30 seconds. Add and stir-fry the masala paste for a further minute.

2 Add the main ingredient or ingredients of your choice and briskly stir-fry it for about 3 minutes.

3 Add the Balti Base Sauce and bring to the simmer.

4 Add the remaining ingredients and aromatic salt to taste. Simmer until it is cooked to your liking. Garnish with kiwi slices and coriander and serve.

BALTI JAL FREZI

— ◆ —

'*Jal frezi*' (also spelt *Jal Frifi* or *Jalfrizi*) means dry stir-fry, which is Balti cooking, almost by definition. Here we achieve lightness of touch by brief cooking and the freshness of the support ingredients – chilli, fresh garlic, ginger, onion, peppers and coriander.

Serves 4 *(makes 4 portions)*

1½ *lb (675 g) main ingredient of your choice (par-cooked meat using the recipe on page 45, or raw poultry cubes, or raw fish or shellfish, or any vegetables from chapter 5, or any combination of main ingredients)*

5 *fl oz (150 ml) Special Balti Base Sauce (see page 108)*

1 *tablespoon ghee or vegetable oil*

2–3 *garlic cloves, finely chopped*

1 *tablespoon green masala paste (see page 39)*

4 *oz (110 g) onion, thinly sliced*

½ *a red pepper cut into small diamond shapes*

½ *a green pepper cut into small diamond shapes*

2–4 *tablespoons fresh coriander leaves, finely chopped*

a squeeze of lemon juice

a sprinkling of Balti garam masala (see page 33)

aromatic salt to taste (see page 34)

some fresh coriander leaves to garnish

SPICES

1½ *teaspoons cummin seed*

½ *teaspoon lovage seeds*

½ *teaspoon coriander seeds*

1 Heat the ghee or oil in the karahi. Stir-fry the **Spices** for 30 seconds then add and stir-fry the garlic for a further 30 seconds. Add and stir-fry the masala paste for a further minute. Add the onion and stir-fry for 3 more minutes.

2 Add the main ingredient or ingredients of your choice and briskly stir-fry it for about 3 minutes.

3 Add the special Balti Base Sauce and bring to the simmer.

4 Add the peppers, chopped coriander, lemon juice and garam masala and simmer until it is cooked to your liking. Add aromatic salt to taste.

5 Garnish with coriander leaves and serve.

BALTI KASHMIRI CURRY

— ♦ —

Most Balti house operators will tell you they come from Pakistan's Kashmir area (if not from Baltisan itself). We've already met some of the area's authentically flavoured dishes, but this one is the Balti house invention. The Special Balti Base Sauce is enhanced with interestingly textured lotus roots and sweet fruits such as lychees with their syrup.

Serves 4 (makes 4 portions)

1¹/₂ lb (675 g) main ingredient of your choice (par-cooked meat using the recipe on page 45, or raw poultry cubes, raw fish or shellfish, or any vegetables from Chapter 5, or any combination of main ingredients)

15 fl oz (450 ml) Special Balti Base Sauce (see page 108)

1 tablespoon ghee or vegetable oil

2–3 garlic cloves, finely chopped

1 tablespoon Balti masala paste (see page 38)

3 oz (75 g) lotus roots

5 oz (150 g) tinned lychees, strained

2 tablespoons juice from the lychees

1 tablespoon dark muscovado sugar

aromatic salt to taste (see page 34)

some fresh coriander leaves to garnish

1 Heat the ghee or oil in the karahi and stir-fry the garlic for 30 seconds. Add and stir-fry the masala paste for a further minute.

2 Add the main ingredient or ingredients of your choice and briskly stir-fry it for about 3 minutes.

3 Add the Special Balti Base Sauce and bring to the simmer.

4 Add the remaining ingredients and aromatic salt to taste. Simmer until it is cooked to your liking. Garnish with coriander leaves and serve.

BALTI KOFTA CURRY

— ♦ —

Koftas are small, spicy meat balls, which are easy to make with this foolproof method, and delicious when floated in Balti curry.

Serves 4 (makes 4 portions)

KOFTAS

$1^1/_4$ lb (550 g) best quality lean meat (any type)

2 garlic cloves, finely chopped

2 tablespoons dehydrated onion flakes

1 tablespoon finely chopped fresh coriander leaves

1 tablespoon Balti masala mix (see page 31)

1 teaspoon Balti garam masala (see page 33)

$^1/_2$ teaspoon salt

BALTI CURRY

15 fl oz (450 ml) Special Balti Base Sauce (see page 108)

1 tablespoon ghee or vegetable oil

2–3 garlic cloves, finely chopped

1 tablespoon Balti masala paste (see page 38)

1 tablespoon tomato purée

6 oz (175 g) tinned tomatoes, strained

1 teaspoon granulated sugar

$^1/_2$ teaspoon dried fenugreek leaf

aromatic salt to taste (see page 34)

some fresh coriander leaves to garnish

TO MAKE THE KOFTAS

1 Coarsely chop the meat, then run it and all the remaining kofta ingredients through a food processor, or twice through a hand mincer, achieving a finely textured paste.

2 Mix the paste thoroughly. Divide it into four equal parts. From each part roll six small balls (koftas).

3 Preheat the oven to 375°F/190°C/Gas 5. Put the 24 koftas on an oven tray and bake them for 15 minutes.

TO MAKE THE BALTI CURRY

4 Heat the ghee or oil in the karahi and stir-fry the garlic for 30 seconds. Add and stir-fry the masala paste for a further minute.

5 Add the koftas and briskly stir-fry for about 3 minutes. Add the Special Balti Base Sauce and bring to the simmer.

6 Add the tomato purée, tomatoes, sugar and fenugreek and salt to taste. Simmer for about 10 minutes or until it is cooked to your liking. Garnish with coriander leaves.

BALTI KORMA
— ♦ —

'Korma' actually describes a method of slow cooking rather than the heat level of a particular dish. In Kashmir they produce a korma bursting with red Kashmiri chillies! However, the aromatic spices, cream, milk and saffron generally mean mild, as here.

Serves 4 *(makes 4 portions)*

1½ lb (675 g) main ingredient of your choice (par-cooked meat using the recipe on page 45, or raw poultry cubes, raw fish or shellfish, or any vegetables from Chapter 5, or any combination of main ingredients)
1 tablespoon ghee or vegetable oil
2–3 garlic cloves, finely chopped
1½ teaspoons Balti masala paste (see page 38)
15 fl oz (450 ml) Special Balti Base Sauce (see page 108)

4 fl oz (120 ml) thick double cream
1 teaspoon sugar
20 whole fried almonds
20 to 25 saffron strands lightly roasted (see page 30)
aromatic salt to taste (see page 34)
some fresh coriander leaves to garnish

SPICES
2 bay leaves
2 in (5 cm) piece cassia bark
4–6 green cardamoms
4–6 cloves

1 Heat the ghee or oil in the karahi. Stir-fry the **Spices** for 30 seconds then add and stir-fry the garlic for a further 30 seconds. Add and stir-fry the masala paste for a further minute.

2 Add the main ingredient or ingredients of your choice and briskly stir-fry for about 3 minutes. Add the Special Balti Base Sauce and bring to the simmer.

3 Add the cream, sugar, almonds, saffron and aromatic salt to taste. Simmer until cooked to your liking. Garnish and serve.

117

BALTI MADRAS

— ♦ —

I doubt that many Balti house owners have ever been to Madras, a major city in southern India, but Balti Madras is much demanded by their clients. This is an interpretation of the hot dishes from that part of the world. It is hot but not searing.

Serves 4 (makes 4 portions)

1¹/₂ lb (675 g) main ingredient of your choice (par-cooked meat using the recipe on page 45, or raw poultry cubes, or raw fish or shellfish, or any vegetables from Chapter 5, or any combination of main ingredients)

1 tablespoon ghee or vegetable oil

2–3 garlic cloves, finely chopped

1 tablespoon mild masala paste (see page 38)

1 tablespoon tandoori masala paste (see page 39)

15 fl oz (450 ml) special Balti Base Sauce (see page 108)

6 oz (175 g) tinned tomatoes, strained

2 tablespoons tomato ketchup

2 tablespoons ground almonds

2 tablespoons dehydrated onion flakes, fried (see page 28)

aromatic salt to taste (see page 34)

some fresh coriander leaves to garnish

SPICES

2–4 teaspoons chilli powder

1 teaspoon ground cummin

1 Heat the ghee or oil in the karahi, stir-fry the **Spices** for 30 seconds then add and stir-fry the garlic for a further 30 seconds. Add and stir-fry the pastes for a further minute.

2 Add the main ingredient or ingredients of your choice and briskly stir-fry for about 3 minutes.

3 Add the Special Balti Base Sauce and bring to the simmer.

4 Add the tomatoes, ketchup, almonds and onion flakes and aromatic salt to taste. Simmer until it is cooked to your liking. Garnish with coriander leaves and serve.

BALTI MALAY CURRY

— ♦ —

Malaysia is jungle country, with images of dense foliage, screeching parrots and howling monkeys. This Balti house recipe includes pineapple in this mild-tasting malay-style dish.

Serves 4 *(makes 4 portions)*

1¹/₂ lb (675 g) main ingredient of your choice (par-cooked meat using the recipe on page 45, or raw poultry cubes, or raw fish or shellfish, or any vegetables from Chapter 5, or any combination of main ingredients)

1 tablespoon ghee or vegetable oil
2–3 garlic cloves, finely chopped

1¹/₂ tablespoons Balti masala paste (see page 38)
7¹/₂ fl oz (225 ml) Special Balti Base Sauce (see page 108)
6–8 chunks fresh or tinned pineapple
aromatic salt to taste (see page 34)
a sprinkling of desiccated coconut to garnish
some fresh coriander leaves to garnish

1 Heat the ghee or oil in the karahi and stir-fry the garlic for 30 seconds. Add and stir-fry the masala paste for a minute.

2 Add the main ingredient or ingredients of your choice and briskly stir-fry for about 3 minutes.

3 Add the Special Balti Base Sauce and bring to the simmer. Add the pineapple and aromatic salt to taste. Simmer until it is cooked to your liking. Garnish with coriander and coconut.

BALTI MOGLAI CURRY

— ♦ —

Not for the calorie conscious, Moglai curries come rich in ghee, cream and aromatics.

Serves 4 *(makes 4 portions)*

$1^1/_2$ *lb (675 g) main ingredient of your choice (par-cooked meat using the recipe on page 45, or raw poultry cubes, or raw fish or shellfish, or any vegetables from Chapter 5, or any combination of main ingredients)*

1 tablespoon ghee or vegetable oil
2–3 garlic cloves, finely chopped
1 tablespoon Balti masala paste (see page 38)
$7^1/_2$ *fl oz (225 ml) Special Balti Base Sauce (see page 108)*
$3^1/_2$ *oz (100 g) raw cashew nuts*
5 fl oz (150 ml) single cream

4 tablespoons Greek yoghurt
20 saffron strands
1 tablespoon finely chopped fresh coriander leaves
2 tablespoons fried dehydrated onion flakes (see page 28)
aromatic salt to taste (see page 34)
melted ghee to garnish
a sprinkling of flaked almonds to garnish
some fresh coriander leaves to garnish

SPICES
2 brown cardamoms
2 star anise
1 teaspoon aniseed
1 teaspoon sesame seed

1 Heat the ghee or oil in the karahi. Stir-fry the **Spices** for 30 seconds, then add and stir-fry the garlic for a further 30 seconds. Add and stir-fry the masala paste for a further minute.

2 Add the main ingredient or ingredients of your choice and briskly stir-fry for about 3 minutes.

3 Mix the nuts, cream and yoghurt in the blender and grind to a fine pourable paste. Add a little water if needed. Add this and the Special Balti Base Sauce to the main ingredients and bring to the simmer.

4 Add the saffron, chopped coriander and onion flakes and aromatic salt to taste. Simmer until it is cooked to your liking.

5 Drizzle with melted ghee, and garnish.

BALTI PATIA

— ◆ —

The original Patia curry came from Persia via the Parsee (ex-Persian) community who now live in Bombay. It is a rich deep-red colour and is sweet and savoury and hottish.

Serves 4 *(makes 4 portions)*

1½ lb (675 g) main ingredients of your choice (par-cooked meat using the recipe on page 45 or raw poultry cubes, or raw fish or shellfish, or any vegetables from Chapter 5, or any combination of main ingredients)

1 tablespoon ghee or vegetable oil
2–3 garlic cloves, finely chopped
2 teaspoons paprika
1–2 teaspoons chilli powder

2 tablespoons tandoori masala paste (see page 39)
7½ fl oz (225 ml) Special Balti Base Sauce (see page 108)
1 tablespoon tomato purée
2 or 3 tomatoes, finely chopped
½ red pepper, very finely chopped
2 teaspoons brown sugar
1 tablespoon vinegar (any type)
aromatic salt to taste (see page 34)
some fresh coriander leaves to garnish

1 Heat the ghee or oil in the karahi. Stir-fry the garlic, paprika and chilli powder for 30 seconds. Add the tandoori masala paste and stir-fry for a further minute.

2 Add the main ingredient or ingredients of your choice and briskly stir-fry for about 3 minutes.

3 Stir in the Special Balti Base Sauce and tomato purée. Add the fresh tomato, red pepper, sugar and vinegar and simmer for at least 5 minutes more and until it is cooked to your liking.

4 Salt to taste and garnish with coriander leaves.

Facing page 120, top to bottom: Red Balti Roti (page 143), Balti Mint Dip (page 147), Bhola Balti (page 129), and Balti Special Chutney (page 146)

Opposite: Balti Mt-Sp-Cha-Chi-Aub (page 135), served with Karak Naan (page 145)

BALTI PHAL

— ♦ —

Simply the hottest possible Balti dish the cook can make – only for serious hot-heads. The tip is to obtain 'extra-hot chilli powder'.

Serves 4 *(makes 4 portions)*

1½ lb (675 g) main ingredients of your choice (par-cooked meat using the recipe on page 45, or raw poultry cubes, or raw fish or shellfish, or any vegetables from Chapter 5, or any combination of main ingredients)

1 tablespoon ghee or vegetable oil

2–3 garlic cloves, finely chopped

4 or more teaspoons extra-hot chilli powder

2 tablespoons tandoori masala paste (see page 39)

7½ fl oz (225 ml) Special Balti Base Sauce (see page 108)

6 oz (175 g) tomato, chopped

4–8 fresh red and/or green chillies, whole or chopped

1 tablespoon vinegar (any type)

aromatic salt to taste (see page 34)

some fresh coriander leaves to garnish

1 Heat the ghee or oil in the karahi. Stir-fry the garlic and chilli powder for 30 seconds. Add and stir-fry the tandoori paste for a further minute.

2 Add the main ingredient or ingredients of your choice and briskly stir-fry for about 3 minutes.

3 Add the Special Balti Base Sauce and bring to the simmer. Add the tomato, fresh chillies and vinegar and aromatic salt to taste. Simmer until cooked to your liking. Garnish with coriander leaves and serve.

BALTI QUETTA EARTHQUAKE

— ♦ —

The Madras, Vindaloo and Phal Balti curries elsewhere in this chapter are hot, hotter and hottest in that order. This Balti stir-fry comes from the same school of (some would say 'wicked') thought.

It uses chillies, chillies and more chillies and must be treated with great respect. It got its name from the great earthquake which devested Quetta in 1935. One of my uncles was there at the time. This version measures plenty on the Richter scale, the actual heat depending on the heat of the chillies and chilli powder (in the masala paste) that you use. It is not to be eaten by the unwary!

Serves 4 *(makes 4 portions)*

1 lb (450 g) main ingredients of your choice (par-cooked meat using the recipe on page 45 or raw poultry cubes, or raw fish or shellfish, or any vegetables from Chapter 5, or any combination of main ingredients)

2 tablespoons ghee or vegetable oil
4–6 garlic cloves, finely chopped

2 tablespoons green masala paste (see page 39)
7½ fl oz (225 ml) Special Balti Base Sauce (see page 108)
8 oz (225 g) red and/or green chillies, de-stalked but left whole
1 tablespoon dry fenugreek leaf
1 tablespoon brown sugar
2 tablespoons chopped fresh coriander leaves
salt to taste
a few raw chillies to garnish

1 Heat the ghee or oil in the karahi. Stir-fry the garlic for 30 seconds. Add the green masala paste and stir-fry for a further minute.

2 Add the main ingredient or ingredients of your choice and briskly stir-fry for about 3 minutes.

3 Add the Special Balti Base Sauce and bring it to the simmer.

4 Add the fresh chillies, fenugreek, sugar, coriander and salt to taste. Simmer until cooked to your liking.

5 Garnish with raw chillies and serve.

BALTI RHOGAN JOSH

— ◆ —

The authentic Rhogan Josh originated in Kashmir at the time of the Moghul Emperors. Literally meaning cooked in ghee in red gravy, it uses aromatic whole spices. The Balti house incorporates red pepper for colour. I've added beetroot (optional) to achieve a gorgeous deep colour.

Serves 4 (makes 4 portions)

1½ lb (657 g) main ingredients of your choice (par-cooked meat using the recipe on page 45, or raw poultry cubes, or raw fish or shellfish, or any vegetables from Chapter 5, or any combination of main ingredients)

1 tablespoon ghee or vegetable oil

2–3 garlic cloves, finely chopped

1 teaspoon tandoori masala paste (see page 39)

15 fl oz (450 ml) Special Balti Base Sauce (see page 108)

1 tablespoon tomato purée

2 tablespoons ground almonds

1 red pepper, seeded and cut into diamonds

2 oz (50 g) fresh beetroot, peeled and shredded

1 tablespoon chopped fresh coriander leaves

aromatic salt to taste (see page 34)

some fresh coriander leaves to garnish

SPICES
6 cloves
2 bay leaves
2 in (5 cm) piece cassia bark
2 brown cardamoms
4 green cardamoms
½ teaspoon black cummin seeds
½ teaspoon paprika

1 Heat the ghee or oil in the karahi. Stir-fry the **Spices** for 30 seconds then add and stir-fry the garlic for a further 30 seconds. Add and stir-fry the tandoori paste for a futher minute.

2 Add the main ingredient or ingredients of your choice and briskly stir-fry for about 3 minutes.

3 Add the Special Balti Base Sauce and bring to the simmer.

4 Add the tomato purée, almonds, pepper, beetroot, chopped coriander and aromatic salt to taste. Simmer until it is cooked to your liking. Garnish with coriander leaves and serve.

BALTI VINDALOO

— ◆ —

The original vindaloo came from the ex-Portuguese colony of Goa in south-west India and involved pork, vinegar, garlic and chillies. You won't find pork on the Balti house menu. Neither does their dish resemble the authentic version, using, as it does, chunks of potato with copious amounts of chilli powder. My recipe here adds a little vinegar and garlic to create a hot but tasty Balti dish.

Serves 4 *(makes 4 portions)*

18 oz (500 g) main ingredient of your choice (par-cooked meat using the recipe on page 45, or raw poultry cubes, or raw fish or shellfish, or any vegetables from Chapter 5, or any combination of main ingredients)

1 tablespoon ghee or vegetable oil
2–4 teaspoons chilli powder
2–3 garlic cloves, finely chopped
2 tablespoons Balti masala paste (see page 38)

15 fl oz (450 ml) Special Balti Base Sauce (see page 108)
3–6 fresh red or green chillies, chopped
1 portion cooked potato in a Balti Spice Base for Vegetables (see pages 98–9 and 90–1)
2 teaspoons dried fenugreek leaf
aromatic salt to taste (see page 34)
some fresh coriander leaves to garnish

1 Heat the ghee or oil in the karahi. Stir-fry the chilli powder for 30 seconds then add and stir-fry the garlic for a further 30 seconds. Add and stir-fry the masala paste for a further minute.

2 Add the main ingredient or ingredients of your choice and briskly stir-fry for about 3 minutes.

3 Add the Special Balti Base Sauce and bring to the simmer.

4 Add the chillies, the potato in Spice Base for Vegetables, and the fenugreek and aromatic salt to taste. Simmer until it is cooked to your liking. Garnish with coriander leaves and serve.

CHAPTER · 7

—◆—

Balti Combination Dishes

'If you can't find your favourite combination on our menu, our chef will be delighted to cook it especially for you', so says the menu for the aptly named **I Am The King of Balti** in Birmingham. With over 60 Balti dishes on the menu you would not imagine more possible combinations could exist. As I've mentioned elsewhere in this book, it is the norm to combine different ingredients and dishes in Balti cooking.

This suits the home cook very well as you can simply use ingredients you have to hand. Balti afficionados call this 'mix-'n'-match'. It means you can serve Balti 'anything' with 'anything'! Balti meat or Balti chicken are perfectly acceptable of course, but so are Balti meat and mushroom or Balti chicken and mushroom. Or you could have Balti meat with mushroom and dhal, or even Balti meat with mushroom, dhal and spinach. I'm sure you've got the picture. The permutations are almost infinite.

Some traditional Balti-house combinations make good reading (and eating!), and I've included them in this chapter. Balti Tropical, for example is equal amounts of meat, chicken and prawns. Balti Tropical Plus adds keema (mince). Balti Tropical Vegetable combines any six vegetables of your choice. Bhola Balti is equal amounts of lamb, chicken and mixed vegetables. I've also included in this chapter, a representative selection of Balti vegetable combinations, the most celebrated of which is **Adil's** Balti Mt-spi-cha-chi-aub. To decode this turn to page 135.

The main thing to keep in mind is the total weight of ingredients. The total approximate weight of all your (raw) principal ingredients should be around $1\frac{1}{2}$ lb (675 g) to serve four people. So in the case of Balti Tropical the raw prepared meat, chicken and prawns will each weigh 8 oz (225 g). Balti Tropical Plus's four items will each weigh 6 oz (17 g) and Balti Mt-spi-cha-chi-aub's five items, approximately 5 oz (150 g) each.

To help you work out quantities, all recipes state how many portions they make. If you only require one portion of a recipe that makes 4 portions, you will find it more practical to cook the complete recipe and freeze the surplus.

Be flexible, be inventive and 'mix-'n'-match' your own combinations of Balti dishes using any items from Chapters 2 to 5. Here, then, are a few examples of what you can combine and how to do it.

BALTI MEAT, POULTRY AND FISH COMBINATIONS

There are six Balti house favourite combinations using meat, poultry and/or fish.

BALTI MEAT AND CHICKEN

— ♦ —

Equal amounts of Balti Meat, Medium Heat and Balti Chicken, Medium Heat. For different flavour combinations you can use any of the meat recipes between pages 46 and 55 and combine them with any of the chicken recipes between pages 66 and 69.

Serves 4 (makes 4 portions)

2 portions Balti Meat, Medium Heat (see page 46)
2 portions Balti Chicken, Medium Heat (see page 66)
salt to taste

some fresh coriander leaves to garnish
Balti garam masala (see page 33) to garnish

Cook the meat and the chicken according to their respective recipes and combine prior to serving. Salt to taste and garnish with the leaves and garam masala.

BALTI TROPICAL

— ♦ —

Equal amounts of Balti Meat, Balti Chicken and Balti Prawns. It sounds fairly bizarre but it works well. The name commonly used in the Balti House is 'Tropical', although why no one can tell me!

Serves 4 *(makes 4 portions)*

$1^1/_3$ *portions Balti Meat,*
  Medium Heat (see page 46)
$1^1/_3$ *portions Balti Chicken,*
  Medium Meat (see page 66)
$1^1/_3$ *portions Balti Prawns (see*
  page 86)

salt to taste
some fresh coriander leaves to
  garnish
Balti garam masala (see page
  33) to garnish

Cook the meat, chicken and prawns according to their respective recipes and combine prior to serving. Salt to taste and garnish with fresh coriander leaves.

BALTI TROPICAL PLUS

— ♦ —

Not for the faint-hearted! This time meat, chicken, prawns and keema are combined in one hearty dish.

Serves 4 *(makes 4 portions)*

1 portion Balti Meat, Medium
  Heat (see page 46)
1 portion Balti Chicken,
  Medium Heat (see page 66)
1 portion Balti Prawns (see page
  86)
1 portion Balti Keema (see page
  56)

salt to taste
pistachio nuts
some fresh coriander leaves to
  garnish
Balti garam masala (see page
  33) to garnish

Cook the meat, chicken, prawns and keema according to their respective recipes and combine prior to serving. Salt to taste and garnish with the nuts, leaves and garam masala.

PRAWNS AND KEEMA

— ◆ —

Equal amounts of Balti Prawns and Balti Keema make a surf'n'turf Balti dish.

Serves 4 *(makes 4 portions)*

2 portions Balti Prawns (see
    page 86)
2 portions Balti Keema (see
    page 56)

salt
some fresh coriander to garnish
Balti garam masala (see page
    33) to garnish

Cook the prawns and keema according to their respective recipes, and combine prior to serving. Salt to taste and garnish with the fresh leaves and garam masala.

BHOLA BALTI

— ◆ —

This recipe is based on one I had at the **Plaza Balti House** in Birmingham's Balsall Heath. It combines lamb, chicken and assorted vegetables. Use any vegetables you like. Here's one suggestion.

Serves 4 *(makes 4 portions)*

1 portion Balti Lamb, Medium
    Heat (see page 46)
1 portion Balti Chicken,
    Medium Heat (see page 66)
1 portion Balti Spice Base for
    Vegetables (see pages 90–1)
6 oz (175 g) mangetout

6 oz (175 g) sweetcorn
salt to taste
some fresh coriander leaves to
    garnish
Balti garam masala (see page
    33) to garnish

1 Prepare and cook the mangetouts and sweetcorn (see page 92), then mix with the Balti Spice Base for Vegetables.

2 Add the Balti lamb and chicken and toss well to combine. Salt to taste and serve piping hot, garnished with leaves and garam masala.

BALTI CHICKEN AND EGG

— ◆ —

All the jokes about which came first have been cracked (excuse the pun) at Lye's **Central Balti House** where this dish is on the menu.

Serves 4 (makes 4 portions)

4 portions Balti chicken,
  Medium Heat (see page 66)
2–4 hardboiled eggs

salt to taste
some fresh coriander leaves to
  garnish

Shell and quarter or halve the eggs and gently stir them into the Balti chicken so that they don't break up. Salt to taste and garnish with coriander leaves. Serve at once.

SOME VEGETABLE COMBINATIONS

The following five recipes give examples of some of the vegetable combinations which are available to you. Equally you can invent your own combinations.

BALTI CHANA ALOO

— ◆ —

A gorgeous combination of gram lentils cooked to a creamy consistency and chunky boiled potato.

Serves 4 (makes 4 portions)

2 portions Balti Gram Lentils
  (see pages 102–3)
2 portions cooked potato in a
  Balti Spice Base for
  Vegetables (see pages 98–9
  and 90–1)
2 tablespoons ghee or vegetable
  oil

5 oz (150 g) yoghurt
aromatic salt to taste (see page
  38)
some fresh coriander leaves to
  garnish
a sprinkling of Balti garam
  masala (see page 33) to
  garnish

1 Heat the ghee or oil in the karahi.

2 Add the Balti gram lentils and, when hot, add the potato in Spice Base for Vegetables and any extra tastes of your choice (see page 91).

3 To keep things mobile, add the yoghurt (it may also need a little water).

4 When heated right through, add aromatic salt to taste and garnish with the coriander leaves and garam masala.

BALTI TOMATO, CELERY, SWEETCORN AND MANGETOUTS
— ♦ —

This is a pretty combination needing lightness of touch, and deft stir-frying.

Serves 4 *(makes 4 portions)*

2 tablespoons ghee or vegetable oil
¹/₃ teaspoon wild onion seeds
¹/₃ teaspoon fennel seeds
¹/₃ teaspoon white cummin seeds
2 garlic cloves, chopped
6 oz (175 g) mangetouts, topped and tailed
6 oz (175 g) small or cherry tomatoes, halved

4 oz (110 g) red and/or green peppers, softened (see page 98)
6 oz (175 g) celery, cooked
aromatic salt to taste (see page 34)
some fresh coriander leaves
20–30 fried cashew nuts, chopped (optional)

1 Heat the ghee or oil in a karahi. Stir-fry the seeds and the garlic for 1 minute.

2 Add the raw mangetouts and briskly stir-fry for 2 minutes, sprinkling in a little water if needed.

3 Now add the tomatoes, and the softened peppers. Once simmering, add the celery, and aromatic salt to taste. Garnish with the leaves and optional nuts, and serve at once.

BALTI LOBIA BEANS, MUSHROOMS AND SPINACH

— ♦ —

This interesting combination makes an attractive, colourful and nutritious dish. Prepare and cook the lobia beans first. Remember that you'll need at least 12 hours to soak the lobia beans, plus 45 minutes to cook them, following the recipe on page 104.

Serves 4 *(makes 4 portions)*

4 portions Balti Spice Base for
   Vegetables (see pages 90–1)
6 oz (175 g) mushrooms
6 oz (175 g) spinach, cooked
2 portions Balti Lobia Beans
  (see page 104)

salt to taste
some fresh coriander leaves to
  garnish
Balti garam masala (see page
  33) to garnish

1 Add the raw mushrooms and the cooked spinach to the Balti Spice Base and bring to a simmer. Add the Balti Lobia Beans and any optional flavouring of your choice (see page 91). Salt to taste and simmer until the mushrooms are cooked.

2 Garnish with the coriander leaves and garam masala and serve.

BALTI VEG-SPI-DAL-CHI

— ♦ —

Otherwise known as mixed vegetables with spinach, dhal and chickpeas, this is the archetypal mix-'n'-match combination beloved by Baltimaniacs. Making up this combination would be lengthy were it not for the freezer. Use frozen mixed vegetables, fresh or frozen spinach, dhal and chickpeas which you've pre-cooked in bulk and frozen in batches (see pages 101 and 103) or for even quicker results used tinned lentils.

Serves 4 *(makes 4 portions)*

1 portion Balti Masoor Lentils (see page 101)
1 portion Balti Chickpeas (see page 103)
1 portion cooked spinach in a Balti Spice Base for vegetables (see pages 99 and 90–1)

6 oz (175 g) frozen mixed vegetables
1 tablespoon ghee or vegetable oil
aromatic salt to taste (see page 34)
some fresh coriander leaves to garnish

1 Heat the ghee or oil in the karahi. Add the Balti masoor lentils and Balti chickpeas and bring to a simmer. Add the mixed vegetables, and return to simmering (If frozen, this will take a while longer.)

2 Add the spinach in Spice Base for Vegetables and any extra tastes of your choice (see page 91). Add a little water if it needs it, and aromatic salt to taste. Serve at once, garnished with the fresh coriander leaves.

BALTI TROPICAL VEGETABLES
— ♦ —

This can be made with equal amounts of any six Balti vegetables of your choice. Here is an example, using a leaf, a bean, a legume, a root, a fruit vegetable and a squash – cauliflower, green beans, red kidney beans, parsnip, tomato and marrow. This particular combination gives a good variety of colour and texture, and makes a very generous main course for four.

Serves 4 (makes 4 portions)

1 portion Balti Red Kidney
  Beans (see page 91)
4 portions Balti Spice Base for
  Vegetables (see pages 90–1)
6 oz (175 g) small cauliflower
  florets
6 oz (175 g) green beans
6 oz (175 g) parsnips, cut into
  bite-sized cubes
6 oz (175 g) tomatoes, chopped

6 oz (175 g) marrow, cut into
  bite-sized pieces
aromatic salt to taste (see page
  34)
some fresh coriander leaves to
  garnish
Balti garam masala (see page
  33) to garnish
some shredded fresh chilli
  (optional), to garnish

1 Make the Balti Red Kidney Beans first, remembering you'll need at least 24 hours to soak them and 45 minutes to cook them.

2 Make the four portions of Balti Spice Base for vegetables by multiplying the quantities of the recipe on pages 90–1 by four.

3 Prepare and/or cook the vegetables according to the A–Z of Vegetables on pages 93–100 then add to the Balti Spice Base along with any optional flavourings of your choice (see page 91).

4 Bring to simmering and add the red kidney beans and aromatic salt to taste.

5 Garnish with the fresh coriander leaves, garam masala and shredded chilli.

COMBINATIONS OF COMBINATIONS

BALTI MT-SPI-CHA-CHI-AUB

— ♦ —

The celebrated dish from Birmingham's popular **Adil's Balti House** (see Introduction). The name above is how it appears on the menu. De-coded it means Balti meat with spinach, chana, chickpeas and aubergine. It's a good, nutritious dish, requiring no more than a Balti naan bread to scoop it up with and a Balti dip to give it zest (see pages 144 and 147). Do not add any additional flavourings to the Balti Spice Base for the aubergine.

Serves 4 *(makes 4 portions)*

1 portion Balti Meat, Medium
  Heat (see page 46)
6 oz (175 g) spinach, cooked
1 portion Balti Gram Lentils
  (see page 102–3)
1 portion Balti Chickpeas (see
  page 103)

1 portion aubergine, cooked
  and in a Spice Base for
  Vegetables (see pages 93 and
  90–1)
salt to taste
some shredded fresh green
  chillies (optinal) to garnish

Combine everything and salt to taste. Garnish and serve hot accompanied by a Balti Naan or Karak Naan.

BALTI EXHAUSTION DISH

— ♦ —

The Ulimate Combination! I mentioned this dish in the Introduction. It is served by at least two well-established Balti houses
and contains anything and everything. 'It will exhaust you eating
it' say the restaurants. Actually it is very popular, and it is a great
way for you to use up left overs. Alternatively serve it as the main
dish at a party.

The recipe here serves eight people, but you could serve it to
fewer and freeze the surplus. Remember too, you can use absolutely
any ingredients, this is just my own suggestion.

Serves 8 *(makes 8 portions)*

*4 portions Balti Tropical Plus
  (see pages 128)*
*4 portions Balti Tropical
  Vegetables (see page 134)*
salt to taste
*toasted flaked almonds to
  garnish*

single cream to garnish
*some fresh coriander leaves to
  garnish*
*Balti garam masala (see page
  33) to garnish*

Combine everything (in two pans if necessary) just prior to serving.
When hot, salt to taste then serve, garnished with nuts, a curl of
cream, fresh coriander and garam masala.

BALTI SIZZLERS

— ♦ —

Balti can be served to the table sizzling and hissing like a snake.
This is a restaurant technique and to do it you'll need to buy
special heavy, steel sizzler Balti pans (see page 17). These come
with a wooden base, and are around 5 in (12.5 cm) in diameter.
They make for attractive presentation of any Balti dish.

Care must be taken not to splatter your guests with boiling oil,
nor to burn them, yourself or your table with the outstandingly
hot Balti bowl.

The technique is simple when you know how. Here are the secrets:

1 The food is cooked to readiness in a separate pan.

2 Just prior to serving place a clean dry Balti bowl directly onto the stove over a ring at its hottest. Let the steel bowl get as hot as it can. It takes at least five minutes.

3 Add a teaspoon or two of ghee or oil in the pan and turn off the heat (to prevent the oil from catching fire).

4 CAREFULLY add half a teaspoon of water or lime juice. Take care, because the hot oil and water will splutter and steam. Add the food at once. Do not load the pan over half full or you may loose the effect. Take to the table, still hissing.

Remember: The pan is blisteringly hot, though still innocently black, so use oven gloves and treat it all with respect!

Any of the Balti recipes or combinations in this book can be served sizzling.

CHAPTER · 8

◆

Accompaniments

Rice is a grain which grows on grass stems in watery fields. The best is Basmati rice, and this grows in the foothills of the Himalayas and in the plains around Kashmir and Baltistan. Wheat grows in the Punjab and Khyber Pass regions so it too is available in the area.

Traditionally either rice or bread was eaten with spicy main dishes, but it is quite acceptable to serve both, plus one or more freshly made raw chutneys or dips. In the Balti houses of Birmingham diners tend to eat bread rather than rice with their Balti. Rice, however, is usually available for those who want it. To discover how to use your bread in place of cutlery see page 23.

PLAIN BOILED RICE

◆

Plain rice is the term the Balti house gives to rice which is simply boiled until tender, but which has no flavouring or colouring added. Personally, I think 'plain' rice is a poor description. No rice is 'plain', and if you use Basmati rice you'll find it has a sumptuous flavour on its own without additions.

A 3 oz (75 g) portion of dry rice provides an ample helping per person; 2 oz (50 g) will be a smaller but adequate portion.

Immersing rinsed dry rice in ample boiling water is the quickest way to cook rice, and it can be ready to serve in just 15 minutes from the water boiling. Two factors are crucial for this method to

138

work perfectly. Firstly, the rice must be Basmati. (Patna or long-grained, quick-cook, or other rices will require different timings and will have neither the texture, the shape nor the fragrance of Basmati.) Secondly, it is one of the few recipes in this book which require precision timing. It is essential that for its few minutes on the boil you concentrate exclusively on it or else it may overcook and became stodgy.

Serves 4 (makes 4 portions)

8–12 oz (225–350 g) Basmati   2–3 pints (1.2–1.75 litres) water
    rice

1 Pick through the rice to remove grit and impurities.

2 Boil the water. It is not necessary to salt it.

3 While the water is heating up, rinse the rice briskly with fresh cold water until most of the starch is washed out. Run hot tap water through the rice at the final rinse. This minimises the temperature reduction when you put the rice into the boiling water.

4 When the water is boiling properly, put the rice into the pan. Start timing. Put the lid on the pan until the water comes back to the boil, then remove the lid. It takes 8–10 minutes from the start. Stir frequently.

5 After about 6 minutes, taste a few grains. As soon as the centre is no longer brittle but still has a good *al dente* bite to it, drain off the water. The rice should seem slightly undercooked.

6 Shake off all the excess water, then place the strainer on to a dry tea towel which will help remove the last of the water.

7 After a minute place the rice in a warmed serving dish. You can serve it now or, preferably, put it into a very low oven or warming drawer for at least 30 minutes and at most 90 minutes. As it dries, the grains will separate and become fluffy.

8 Just before serving, fluff up the rice with a fork to aerate it and release the steam.

COLOURING RICE

— ♦ —

Undoubtedly rice is greatly enhanced in appearance by colouring. Here are three methods:

Saffron
Authentically this is done in Kashmir by using saffron strands from the crocus which is native to Kashmir. Simply add 20–30 strands to your rice at the end of stage 6 of the previous recipe.

Turmeric
This also colours rice, but it will not mix satisfactorily after cooking. It must be added to the boiling water at stage 2 of the above recipe. Use $^1/_8$–$^3/_4$ teaspoon turmeric to obtain evenly coloured grains of rice ranging from pale lemon to orange, depending on how much you use.

Artificial Food Colouring
Known as tartrazine, this is readily available in tiny bottles. Red, orange, yellow and green are suitable for colouring rice. Blue, pink and violet colours are also available, although they are somewhat strange when applied to Balti rice.
Dilute $^1/_2$ teaspoon of liquid colouring with 2 teaspoons water and sprinkle it on to the rice at stage 7 of the previous recipe after you have put the rice into the warmed serving dish. Do not stir it in until stage 8. Use more than one colour if you wish. Do not overlap them when sprinkling.

BALTI FRIED RICE

— ♦ —

Rice absorbs flavours easily, resulting in an exceptionally fine accompaniment to Balti dishes.
This recipe uses plain rice cooked by boiling as described in the recipe on pages 138–9. It takes just a few seconds to flavour the rice. This Balti version is highly aromatic, containing ground spices rather than their chewy whole counterparts found in the traditional rices of Pakistan and India.

Serves 4 (makes 4 portions)

8–12 oz (225–350 g) Basmati rice, cooked to the end of stage 6 of the previous recipe (or it can be cold)	SPICES (ground)
	1 teaspoon sesame seeds
	1 teaspoon Balti garam masala (see page 33)
1 tablespoon unsalted butter, or ghee	*½ teaspoon aniseed*
	¼ teaspoon black cummin seeds
	¼ teaspoon lovage seeds

1 Heat the butter or ghee in the karahi, and stir-fry the ground **Spices** for a few seconds.

2 Add the hot drained or cold rice to the karahi.

3 Mix well and stir-fry until it is warm. Serve now or, preferably, put it into a very low oven or warming drawer for at least 30 minutes and up to 90 minutes. As it dries, the grains will separate and become fluffy.

BALTI BREADS

The indigenous breads of Baltistan and Kashmir are those found all over the sub-continent. They are made from a brown flour called *ata* or *chupatti* flour, which is finely milled from hard grains of wheat and is high in gluten. The breads are always flat discs. I give two types here: the Balti Roti which is unleavened (that is to say, it has no rising agent) and the Balti Naan which is leavened (it contains a rising agent which makes the bread puffier than the roti, although still flat).

The distinctive feature of bread at the Balti house seems to be size. One wonders indeed if there is a competition amongst the chefs to see who can cook the largest. At Birmingham Sparkbrook's **Royal Al Faisal Balti House**, the naans come in three sizes: small (usually about 8 in/20 cm in diameter), medium (large dinner-plate size) and 'family-size' which is brought to the table between two baskets and is literally 3 x 1½ feet (1 x 0.5 metre) in size!

For fun I've given medium to large Balti breads here. Unusual shapes are another feature. Triangles, squares or quadrilateral shapes are all served. Choose your own shape.

BALTI ROTI

— ◆ —

Roti simply means 'bread' and this version is indeed simple to make. It uses wholemeal flour (you can use *ata* flour if available) and will only take you a few minutes to 'knock-up' the dough and less time to cook. You can dry-fry it or fry in a little ghee.

Makes 2 roti *(each large enough to serve 2 people)*

1 lb (450 g) wholemeal or   lukewarm water
    brown ata flour

1 Choose a large ceramic or glass bowl and put in the flour.

2 Add lukewarm water little by little, and work it into the flour with your fingers. Soon it will become a lump.

3 Remove it from the bowl and knead it with your hands on a floured board or work top until the lump is cohesive and well combined.

4 Return it to the bowl and leave it for 10–15 minutes, then briefly knead it once more. It will then be ready to use in the recipes.

5 Divide the dough into two equal lumps.

6 Shape each lump into a ball, then on a floured work surface, roll each ball into a thin disc about 10 in (25 cm) in diameter.

7 Heat a flat pan on a medium heat. When it is at full heat, place one roti on the pan and dry-fry it for about 1 minute or so, until it begins to brown. Press it down (carefully!) with your fingers. Turn it over and cook the other side.

8 Repeat with the other roti, serve promptly and just prior to serve dab over your naked gas or electric ring (not ceramic hob). This will enhance and encourage the brown spots to develop and enable you to serve the rotis piping hot.

GREEN BALTI ROTI

— ♦ —

This stunning roti is naturally green. Simply add fresh puréed green herbs and vegetables to the dough.

Makes 2 roti *(each large enough to serve 2 people)*

1 lb (450 g) wholemeal or
  brown ata flour
lukewarm water

FOR THE PURÉE
2 tablespoons chopped fresh
  coriander leaves
2 tablespoons chopped fresh
  mint

1 tablespoon green masala
  paste (see page 33)
1 tablespoon chopped frozen
  spinach leaf
1 teaspoon aromatic salt (see
  page 34)
0–2 fresh green chillies, finely
  chopped (optional)

1 Mulch down the purée ingredients in the blender, using sufficient water to achieve a smooth easily pourable purée. Add to the dry flour at stage 1 of the previous recipe, then follow stages 2 to 8 of that recipe.

RED BALTI ROTI

— ♦ —

This alternative red version of the basic roti is very tasty.

1 lb (450 g) whole meal or
  brown ata flour
hot water

FOR THE PURÉE
2 tablespoons tomato purée
1 tablespoon tandoori masala
  paste (see page 39)

2 tablespoons finely chopped
  red pepper (seeded first)
2 tablespoons finely chopped
  tomato (seeded first)
0–2 teaspoons chilli powder
  (optional)

1 Mulch down the purée ingredients in the blender, using sufficient water to achieve a smooth, easily pourable purée. Add to the dry flour at stage 1 of the recipe opposite, then follow stages 2 to 8 of that recipe.

BALTI NAAN

— ◆ —

The original version of the naan and the oven it is cooked in, the tandoor, were brought to the North-West Frontier by the Ancient Persians, who called them respectively *nane* and *tonir*. So they are a traditional staple food for Baltis and Kashmiris. The transition to the Balti house was a natural progression.

As with the rotis, they can be quite large. This method uses the grill and it produces a huge, light, fluffy, slightly sweet and chewy, mouth-watering bread. The traditional tear-shape comes about because the bread is pressed on to the neck of the tandoor, and gravity causes it to elongate to that shape. You can simulate it in this recipe, or alternatively cut it to a square, triangular or rectangular shape.

Makes 2 Balti naan (each large enough to serve 2 people)

1 lb (450 g) strong white flour
1 tablespoon baking powder
1 tablespoon granulated sugar
2 tablespoons Greek yoghurt
1 teaspoon aromatic salt (see page 34)

2 teaspoons sesame seeds
$^{1}/_{2}$ teaspoon wild onion seed
lukewarm water
a little ghee, melted

1 Choose a large ceramic or glass bowl and put in all the ingredients except the ghee.

2 Add warm water little by little and work it into the flour with your fingers. Soon it will become a lump.

3 Remove from the bowl and knead on a floured board until well combined. Return to the bowl and leave in a warm place for a couple of hours to prove.

4 Your dough, when risen, should have doubled in size. It should be bubbly, stringy and elastic.

5 Knock back the dough by kneading it down to its original size.

6 Divide the dough into two equal lumps.

7   Shape each lump into a ball, then on a floured work surface, roll each ball into a disc about 12 in (25 cm) in diameter. It should be at least $^1/_4$ in (5 mm) thick. If you wish you can elongate one end so that it achieves the traditional tear shape.

8   Preheat the grill to three-quarters heat, cover the rack with foil, and set it in the midway position.

9   Put the naan on the foil and grill it. Watch it cook (it can easily burn). As soon as the first side develops brown patches, remove it from the grill.

10   Turn it over and brush the uncooked side with a little melted ghee.

11   Return to the grill and cook until sizzling. Remove.

12   Repeat stages 9–11 with the other naan. Serve at once.

KARAK NAAN
— ◆ —

Amongst certain of the Birmingham Balti houses there seems to be a competition as to who can produce the largest naan breads. They call them Karak, Kharri or Jandala Naan.

To make one Karak Naan, simply follow the above Balti Naan recipe, but use all the dough to roll out only one large tear-drop shape. It will be about 20 x 12 in (50 x 30 cm) and will be quite difficult to handle. Place it on a foil-lined grill or oven pan and cook as in the previous recipe.

CHUTNEY, SALAD AND DIPS

BALTI SPECIAL CHUTNEY
— ♦ —

This is colourful and acidic, and extremely good for you with its high raw onion content. I am often asked how the restaurants obtain its translucent appearance. Here's the secret!

Serves 4

6–8 oz (175–225 g) onion, thinly sliced

3 or 4 cherry tomatoes, quartered

1 green chilli, finely chopped (optional)

1 teaspoon bottled vinegared mint

1 tablespoon coarsely chopped fresh coriander leaves

juice of 1 lemon

aromatic salt to taste (see page 34)

chopped red pepper or chilli to garnish (optional)

Mix everything together. You can serve it immediately, but if you cover it and let it stand in the fridge for between 24 and 48 hours, the onion marinates in the juices, absorbs the flavours, and becomes translucent. Garnish, if liked, and serve.

BALTI SALAD
— ♦ —

This lightly spiced salad is the perfect foil to rich food. The choice of ingredients is up to you, but I've included some unusual things to make your salad interesting and a talking point.

Serves 4

2 tablespoons sesame oil

1 teaspoon mustard seeds

1/2 teaspoon wild onion seeds

1 garlic clove, chopped

2 oz (50 g) white cabbage leaves, shredded

2 oz (50 g) fresh spinach leaves, chopped

2 oz (50 g) celeriac, shredded

1 carrot, shredded

1 courgette, finely sliced

6–8 mangetouts, sliced

0–2 fresh green and/or red chillies, chopped into rings (optional)

aromatic salt to taste (see page 34)

lemon juice to taste

1 Heat the oil in your Karahi, and stir-fry the seeds for 10 seconds then the garlic for a further 30 seconds. Allow to go cold.

2 Mix the cold flavoured oil and the prepared vegetables in a large bowl, and salt to taste. Chill until required.

3 Serve with a liberal squeeze of lemon juice.

BALTI DIP
— ◆ —

This yoghurt-based sauce takes but a minute to make, and goes perfectly with Balti dishes.

Serves 4

5 oz (150 g) Greek yoghurt
1 teaspoon tandoori masala
   paste (see page 39)

$^1/_2$ teaspoon Balti garam masala
   (see page 33)

Simply whisk together with a fork and serve chilled.

BALTI MINT DIP
— ◆ —

This is a variation of the previous recipe, using fresh mint and yoghurt.

Serves 4

5 oz (150 g) Greek yoghurt

2 tablespoons finely chopped
   fresh mint

Simply whisk together with a fork and serve chilled.

Appendix 1

— ◆ —

THE CURRY CLUB

Pat Chapman always had a deep-rooted interest in spicy food, curry in particular, and over the years he built up a huge pool of information which he felt could be usefully passed on to others. He conceived the idea of forming an organisation for this purpose.

Since it was founded in January 1982, **The Curry Club** has built up a membership of several thousands. We have a marchioness, some lords and ladies, knights a-plenty, a captain of industry or two, generals, admirals and air marshals (not to mention a sprinkling of ex-colonels), and we have celebrity names – actresses, politicians, rock stars and sportsmen. We have an airline (Air India), a former R.N. warship (HMS *Hermes*) and a hotel chain (the Taj group).

We have 15 members whose name is Curry or Currie, 20 called Rice, and several with the name Spice or Spicer, Cook, Fry, Frier, or Fryer, and one Boiling. We have a Puri (a restaurant owner), a Paratha and a Nan, a good many Mills and Millers, one Dal and a Lentil, an Oiler, a Gee (but no Ghee), and a Butter but no Marj (several Majories though, and a Majoram and a Minty). We also have several Longs and Shorts, Thins and Broads, one Fatt and one Wide, and a Chilley and a Coole.

We have members on every continent, including a good number of Asian members, but by and large the membership is a typical cross-section of the Great British Public, ranging in age from teenage to dotage, and in occupation from refuse collectors to receivers, high-street traders to high-court judges, tax inspectors to taxi drivers. There are students and pensioners, millionaires and unemployed ... thousands of people who have just one thing in common – a love of curry and spicy foods.

Members receive a bright and colourful magazine four times a year, which has regular features on curry and the curry lands. It includes news items, recipes, reports on restaurants, picture features and contributions from members and professionals alike. The information is largely concerned with curry, but by popular demand it now includes regular input on other exotic and spicy cuisines such as those of the Middle East and China. We have produced a wide selection of publications, including the books listed on page ii, all published by Piatkus. There is also a cookery video.

Obtaining the ingredients required for Indian, Oriental and Middle Eastern cooking can be difficult, but The Curry Club makes it easy, with a comprehensive range of Curry Club products, including spice mixes, chutneys, pickles, papadoms, sauces and curry pastes. These are available from major food stores and specialist delicatessens up and down the country. If they are not stocked near you, there is the Club's well-established and efficient mail-order service. Hundreds of items are stocked, including spices, pickles, pastes, dry foods, tinned foods, gift items, publications and specialist kitchen and tableware.

On the social side, the Club holds residential weekend cookery courses and gourmet nights to selected restaurants.

Top of the list is our regular Curry Club Gourmet trip to India and other spicy countries. We take a small group of curry enthusiasts to the chosen country and tour the incredible sights, in between sampling the delicious foods of each region.

If you would like more information about The Curry Club, write (enclosing a SAE) to: **The Curry Club, PO Box 7, Haslemere, Surrey GU27 1EP.**

Appendix 2

— ◆ —

THE STORE CUPBOARD

Here is a workable list of items you need to make the recipes in this book, subdivided into essential and non-essential. The essential items appear again and again in the recipes, the non-essential appear only in one or two. This list may look a bit formidable but remember, once you have the items in stock they will last for some time. I have listed in metric only as most of the packaging these days *is* metric only.

All items listed are available in the quantities stated, by post from The Curry Club (see Appendix 1 for address).

ESSENTIAL WHOLE SPICES

Bay leaves	4 g
Cardamom, black or brown	15 g
Cardamom, green or white	15 g
Cassia bark	6 g
Chillies	5 g
Cloves	13 g
Coriander seeds	13 g
Cummin seeds, white	18 g
Curry leaves, dry	4 g
Fennel seeds	15 g
Fenugreek leaves, dry	4 g
Mustard seeds	35 g
Peppercorns, black	2 g
Sesame seeds, white	29 g
Wild onion seeds	28 g

NON-ESSENTIAL GROUND SPICES

Asafoetida	40 g
Cardamom, green	18 g

Cassia bark	20 g
Cloves	18 g
Mango Powder	25 g

ESSENTIAL GROUND SPICES

Black pepper	22 g
Chilli powder	20 g
Coriander	16 g
Cummin	16 g
Garam masala	23 g
Paprika	20 g
Turmeric	21 g

ESSENTIAL DRY FOODS

Basmati rice	500 g
Coconut Powder	50 g
Gram flour	500 g
Masoor (red) lentils	500 g

NON-ESSENTIAL WHOLE SPICES

Cummin seeds, black	20 g
Fenugreek seeds	36 g

Lovage seeds	50 g
Nutmeg, whole	10 g
Panch phoran	20 g
Saffron stamens	$\frac{1}{2}$ g

NON-ESSENTIAL DRY FOODS

Food colouring powder, red (beetroot powder)	25 g
Food colouring powder, yellow (annatto)	25 g
Lentils –	
Channa, split	500 g
Chick peas	500 g
Lobia beans (black eyed)	500 g
Nuts –	
Almond, whole	50 g
Cashew	100 g
Pistachio	100 g
Papadoms, spiced and plain (pack)	300 g
Red kidney beans	500 g

INDEX